IMAGES
of Aviation

MacDill Air Force Base

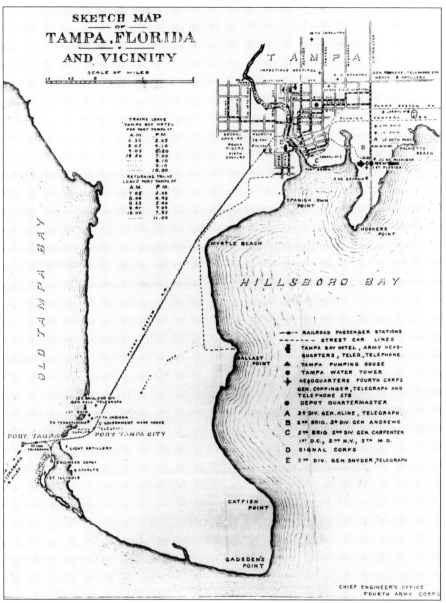

This is a sketch map drawn in 1898 and reproduced in March 1935 depicting the locations of US Army encampments in and around the Tampa area. Catfish Point and Gadsden's Point (bottom) represent the area that would later become MacDill Field. The location where Roosevelt's Rough Riders bivouacked prior to their departure for Cuba during the Spanish-American War can be seen in the upper portion of the picture. (Courtesy Hillsborough County Public Library System, Burgert Brothers Collection.)

ON THE COVER: MacDill Field's formal dedication ceremony took place on the flight line at 3:00 p.m. on April 16, 1941. The event was open to the public, who enjoyed reviewing B-18A Bolos and A-17 Nomad bombers; P-36, P-37, and P-40 pursuit fighters; and B-17 Flying Fortresses. Visitors toured MacDill's completed hangars, which contained armament and ordnance displays, including tail guns, twin-.50s, and 2,000-pound bombs. (Courtesy author.)

IMAGES
of Aviation

MacDill Air Force Base

Steven A. Williamson

ARCADIA
PUBLISHING

Copyright © 2011 by Steven A. Williamson
ISBN 978-0-7385-8775-2

Published by Arcadia Publishing
Charleston, South Carolina

Printed in the United States of America

Library of Congress Control Number: 2011922214

For all general information, please contact Arcadia Publishing:
Telephone 843-853-2070
Fax 843-853-0044
E-mail sales@arcadiapublishing.com
For customer service and orders:
Toll-Free 1-888-313-2665

Visit us on the Internet at www.arcadiapublishing.com

*For our service members and civilians on MacDill—past and present—
thank you for taking the fight to the enemy*

CONTENTS

Acknowledgments

The quality of the content you will find in the following pages could not have been achieved without the dedicated assistance and insights of William R. Polson, MacDill's 6th Air Mobility Wing (AMW) historian. His incredible support was instrumental in the completion of this book, and he provided me with a tremendous amount of substance, guidance, and expertise. I would also like to thank T.Sgt. Jennifer A. Lindsey, non-commissioned officer in charge, Secretary of the Air Force Public Affairs Engagement Office, and Lt. Mark Graff, 6th AMW Public Affairs Office, for approving the project and assisting along the way. Many thanks also to Jennifer Dietz and Travis Puterbaugh of the Tampa Bay History Center; Andrew Huse of University of South Florida's Special Collections; Ron Kolwak of the *Tampa Tribune*; the entire staff of the Hillsborough County Public Library System's Burgert Brothers Collection; and University of Tampa's Art Bagley, who provided me with the idea to hunt down old MacDill postcards. Special thanks also to Lindsay Harris Carter, my senior acquisitions editor at Arcadia Publishing, who made my first skirmish into the field of publishing a truly smooth and enjoyable experience; my wonderful parents, Bill and Linda Williamson; and our men and women in uniform, who were the inspiration behind this book.

The images in this volume appear courtesy of MacDill's 6th Air Mobility Wing History Office (6 AMW/HO); Tampa Bay History Center (TBHC); the University of South Florida, Tampa Campus, Special Collections, Hampton Dunn Collection (USF); Hillsborough County Public Library System, Burgert Brothers Collection (HCPL); me (author); and the *Tampa Tribune*.

The author holds a bachelor's degree in English and American literature from the University of South Florida (Tampa campus) and a master's degree in military history from Norwich University (Northfield, Vermont).

INTRODUCTION

For 70 years, local Tampa Bay residents have been enjoying the sweet sounds of freedom in the form of bombers, fighters, and aerial refueling tankers thundering into and out of MacDill Air Force Base (AFB). Hosted by the 6th Air Mobility Wing (AMW), aircraft currently assigned to the base include the Boeing KC-135 Stratotankers of the 91st Air Refueling Squadron (ARS) and the 927th Air Refueling Wing (ARW); the 310th Airlift Squadron's Gulfstream V C-37As; and NOAA's "Hurricane Hunter" Lockheed WP-3D Orions and Gulfstream IVs (which track and bombard a different kind of aerial menace). Various multiservice jet fighters and A-10 Thunderbolt IIs, utilizing the MacDill-based facilities of the 23rd Wing Detachment 1 Unit Complex (DUC), a unit assigned to Moody Air Force Base, can also be observed streaking through the skies to bombard and strafe ground targets at the Avon Park Air Force Range. MacDill's war-fighters are not all borne of the skies, however, as MacDill's tenant units include America's two premier combatant commands: US Central Command (USCENTCOM) and US Special Operations Command (USSOCOM). US Special Operations Command Central (USSOCCENT), which serves as CENTCOM's special operations contingent and which spearheaded America's infiltration of US Special Forces into Northern Afghanistan following the terrorist attacks of September 11, 2001, is also headquartered on MacDill. Other major war-fighting units include Marine Corps Forces Central Command (MARCENT), the Joint Communications Support Element (JCSE), the Florida Air National Guard's 290th Joint Communications Support Squadron (JCSS), and a component of the Naval Reserve Forces Command, Navy Operational Support Center Tampa.

As Hitler's armored divisions and Luftwaffe swept across Europe, in January 1939, the US War Department appointed a commission to screen suitable locations for the establishment of six new Army air bases to be strategically positioned throughout the country, one of which was to be constructed in the Southeast. Envisioning the major role airpower would play in future conflicts and desiring a location within close proximity to the Panama Canal, Caribbean, and Southeast Atlantic coast, the War Department originally favored locating the base in Arcadia, Florida, where a by-then deserted air base had been established during World War I to train military pilots for war. Tampa mayor Robert E. Lee Chancey had different designs, however, and formed a committee of influential real estate barons, local businessmen, and city and county commissioners to convince the War Department to select Tampa as the future location of the proposed air base. After conferring with pilots who had flown maneuvers over the area in May 1938, Gen. Malin Craig, the US Army's chief of staff, and Gen. George C. Marshall, who later succeeded him, provided favorable feedback to the War Department, and Mayor Chancey's persistent lobbying efforts eventually paid off. In May 1939, the War Department quietly took possession of the title for the land located at the southernmost tip of Tampa's Interbay Peninsula, an area that had been referred to as Gadsden's Point and Catfish Point dating back to the time of the Seminole Indian Wars. On July 13, 1939, Gen. Thomas T. Handy, a member of the War Department's General Staff, made the official announcement that Tampa would become the location for the Southeast Air

Base. Mayor Chancey had been notified of the decision the previous day. The following month, in August 1939, Col. Clarence L. Tinker, who at the time was serving as the chief of supply for the Army Air Corps (commonly referred to as the Army Air Force, or AAF, by 1943), made a personal inspection of the site and appointed Lt. Col. Lynwood B. Jacobs to assume command of the massive construction project.

Initial construction funds of just over $3 million were authorized for the base through the Wilcox Act of 1935, and an army quartermaster company of 22 men arrived in Tampa on September 5, 1939, to begin coordinating the construction efforts. Establishing an office on the fourth floor of Tampa's city hall and storing their furniture and equipment in two railroad cars, the men were responsible for surveying the land, taking soil samples, and creating topographical maps before the land-clearing operation could commence. On November 28, 1939, the first contingent of 60 Works Progress Administration (WPA) crewmen arrived and began the arduous task of clearing roughly 3,000 acres of swampy, snake-infested palmetto scrubs into what would later become the largest heavy bombardment air base in the Southeast. On November 30, 1939—just two days later—Secretary of War Harry H. Woodring announced his decision to rename the base MacDill Field in honor of Col. Leslie MacDill, a visionary Army Air Corps officer who perished in a plane crash on November 9, 1938.

The first company of soldiers arrived on MacDill on March 11, 1940, and consisted of the 27th Air Base Group from Barksdale Field, Louisiana. The 27th would later be redesignated the 28th Headquarters and Air Base Squadron and become MacDill Field's host unit. The first troops to arrive were housed in old customs and quarantine buildings that had been utilized by the Port of Tampa's immigration office, at the time the only solid structures on MacDill. Shortly thereafter, on May 15, 1940, MacDill Field received its first tactical unit, the 29th Bombardment Group (Heavy), from Langley Field, Virginia, bringing MacDill's total number of assigned personnel to over 1,000. The 29th arrived equipped with three Boeing B-17 Flying Fortresses, nine Douglas B-18 Bolos, and two Northrop A-17 Nomad bombers. Accompanying the 14 planes, the unit included three officers and 350 enlisted personnel and reported to Colonel Tinker, who had taken command of MacDill on May 17, 1940. With MacDill's runways still under construction, however, the planes and crewmen of the 29th were temporarily bivouacked at Tampa's Drew Field, a small municipal airfield that would later become Tampa International Airport. This arrangement lasted until January 14, 1941, when MacDill's runways were completed and recently promoted Brigadier General Tinker swooped in piloting a B-18, landing the first bomber on MacDill Field. The base was formally dedicated on April 16, 1941, and a host of dignitaries, as well as thousands of local revelers, attended to participate in guided tours and view the birds of war.

On August 13, 1941, the 3rd Bomber Command was activated on MacDill with the responsibility of supervising the tactical training of all bombardment bases within the Third Air Force. Under the 3rd Bomber Command, this task belonged to the Operational Training Units (OTUs), who churned out thousands of highly trained, combat-ready pilots, gunners, engineers, mechanics, radio operators, navigators, and bombardiers. The OTUs on MacDill helped train and staff America's 15 numbered air forces. By the summer of 1944, MacDill's mission transitioned to Replacement Training Units (RTUs), responsible for preparing replacement personnel for overseas units suffering from attrition. The 3rd Bomber Command also had jurisdictional responsibilities for 13 Southeastern states. It was directly responsible for operations for two subordinate bases—Drane Field in Lakeland, Florida, and Henderson Field (also known as Hillsborough Field), located near what would later become Busch Gardens—and three auxiliary bases—in Bonita Springs, Immokalee, and Punta Gorda, Florida. MacDill's hangars and maintenance depots also serviced bombers from Army air fields in Sarasota, Pinellas, Avon Park, and Bartow, Florida, as well as those stationed at Tampa's Drew Field.

The combat crews on MacDill were trained using B-17 Flying Fortresses until June 1, 1942, when the base received Martin B-26 Marauders and was redesignated from a heavy to a medium bombardment base. At the time, the Marauder was the fastest plane of its kind in the world, and the first Marauder to land on MacDill was piloted by none other than Maj. Gen. Jimmy Doolittle, the architect and leader of the famous carrier-borne Doolittle Raid over Tokyo. The Marauders remained MacDill's mainstay until November 6, 1943, when the Flying Fortresses returned to MacDill, and the training mission was transferred from the 21st Bombardment Group to the 488th Bombardment Group. Surrounded on three sides by water, and because of its wide concrete runways and sprawling 5,700 acres of land, MacDill quickly assumed the reputation of being one of the best air bases in the country, if not the world, offering pilots excellent unobstructed visibility during approaches and takeoffs. In 1944, an Inspector General report to the Army Air Force gave MacDill the highest rating possible for an Army installation—Excellent.

Prior to and during World War II, MacDill Field was also engaged in the integration of women and African Americans into base operation and engineering units. The 810th Engineer Aviation Battalion (EAB), an all–African American unit, was activated on MacDill on June 26, 1941, and received six months of training on the use of heavy equipment for constructing roads, bridges, runways, and forward airdromes. Following the Japanese attack on Pearl Harbor, the 810th EAB, joined by the 811th (a later addition), were deployed on January 23, 1942, to the South Pacific, becoming the first two African American aviation engineering units to deploy overseas from the United States. Prior to their departure, Company A of the 810th was responsible for resurrecting Mullet Key (located at the mouth of Tampa Bay), the home of an abandoned fort from the Spanish-American War. Occupied by Union troops to monitor blockade-runners during the Civil War, Mullet Key was transformed by the 810th into MacDill's primary bomb and gunnery range, opening for business on September 8, 1941. Under the Third Air Force, on March 18, 1943, the 927th Engineer Aviation Regiment, an additional all–African American unit, was activated on MacDill Field. Trained as both expert engineers and infantrymen, the units became known as the "fighting engineers" and specialized in ordnance and armaments, demolition work, building forward airdromes, and reconstructing devastated airfields—thus increasing the mobility and advancement of the AAF on the fronts. After excelling at every task they faced, and as the demand for their services grew, the 927th was succeeded by a larger organization named the 3rd Engineer Aviation Unit Training Center (EAUTC), also headquartered on MacDill. Later renamed the 316th Army Air Force Base Unit/EAUTC, the unit trained and staffed African American engineering outfits that saw combat throughout every theater of war.

On April 27, 1943, MacDill received its first contingent of members of the Women's Army Auxiliary Corps (WAACs), including three officers and 250 enlisted personnel. The WAACs formed two companies on MacDill—the 711th WAAC Company, which was designated the Post Headquarters Company, and the 653rd Photo Lab Company, later attached to the 3rd Mapping Squadron. WAACs were represented in virtually every office throughout the base, resided in standard Army barracks, and were responsible for abiding by the usual forms of Army drills and discipline. Strictly off limits to the eyes of MacDill's interested men, the WAAC living quarters area had its own beauty parlor, recreational rooms, miniature Post Exchange, and kitchen staff. By October 1943, Congress had passed a law fully incorporating the Women's Army Auxiliary Corps into the Army, and the organization was redesignated the Women's Army Corps (WACs).

With the cessation of World War II hostilities, MacDill was assigned to the newly formed Strategic Air Command (SAC). It assumed the mission of transitional training in Boeing B-29 Superfortresses under the 307th Bombardment Group (later Wing), which continued until 1951. At that time, MacDill received Boeing KC-97 Stratotankers and the new jet-powered Boeing B-47 Stratojets, and its mission under SAC evolved into one of aerial refueling and strategic bombardment and deterrence under the 6th Air Division and the 305th, 306th, and 307th Bombardment Wings, which continued for over a decade. When the Korean War began, MacDill deployed its 307th to the theater, becoming one of the first Air Force bases to deploy its forces to the war. US Strike Command (USSTRICOM), a joint task force, was established on MacDill on October 9, 1961. STRICOM had operational control over more than a quarter of a million soldiers spread across eight US Army combat divisions, more than 70 Tactical Air Command squadrons, and numerous other combat support units. Directed by the Joint Chiefs of Staff, STRICOM was tasked with deploying highly mobile combat packages anywhere in the world within hours of notice to respond to global emergencies or reinforce regional combatant commands.

On July 1, 1962, with the activation of the 836th Air Division and the 12th and 15th Tactical Fighter Wings, MacDill's mission again became one of training war-fighters. By 1963 an asset of the Tactical Air Command (TAC), part of MacDill's mission was to serve as the USAF's long-range mobile nuclear and conventional tactical strike force. On February 4, 1963, MacDill became the first base in the USAF to receive the new McDonnell F-4 Phantom II aircraft. The first two F-4C variants delivered to the USAF were to Tactical Air Command's 4453rd Combat Crew Training Squadron, based on MacDill, on November 16, 1963. On November 18, 1963, four days before he was assassinated, President Kennedy was on hand at MacDill for a visit and to give two speeches in Tampa. By March 1965, MacDill had also become the first base in the USAF to have two operationally ready F-4C Phantom II wings assigned. The 56th Tactical Fighter Wing (later redesignated the 56th Tactical Training Wing) assumed the role of MacDill's host unit 10 years later. In 1979, it was under the 56th that MacDill received the General Dynamics F-16 Fighting Falcons, which could be seen roaring through Tampa's skies for the next 15 years.

In the air over Fortress Europe and the South Pacific, the A Shau Valley and Khe Sanh, or on the ground in Fallujah, the Hindu Kush, or Mazar-e Sharif, MacDill's conventional and special operations forces—air borne or otherwise—have been punching America's enemies in the jaw since whistling packages first rained down on Pearl Harbor. It is an understatement to suggest that MacDill's war-fighters have represented the very best that America has to offer—and if the moniker "national hero" could also be attached to an inanimate object, MacDill Air Force Base would clearly lead that list.

One

THE SLEEPING GIANT

Forward-thinking statesmen and military theorists in the late 1930s saw the threat looming in Europe and knew America was not prepared for war. The enormous excavation and construction effort required to build MacDill Field was spearheaded by thousands of skilled and unskilled laborers from the Works Progress Administration (WPA). The WPA, which was a public works program under Pres. Franklin Delano Roosevelt's New Deal, employed millions of previously unemployed Americans throughout the 1930s and early 1940s. It was WPA crews who first broke ground on MacDill, known at the time as the Southeast Air Base, on November 28, 1939, and by the time the new base was dedicated on April 16, 1941, the WPA had used $3,159,149 in congressionally appropriated funds to clear thousands of acres of dense vegetation and establish runways and living quarters. During the height of the construction effort, over 2,600 WPA crewmen were assigned to the field, and by the time the runways were completed in 1941, the workers had excavated 1,757,557 cubic yards of earth.

Col. Leslie MacDill was born February 18, 1889, in Monmouth, Illinois, and was commissioned a second lieutenant in 1912 in the Army's Coast Artillery Corps. He received the rating of junior military aviator after completing flight training on July 2, 1915, at the Signal Corps Aviation School in San Diego, California, which at the time served as the Army Air Corps. During World War I, MacDill served as commander of the Aerial Gunnery School at St. Jean de Monte, France. MacDill held a doctorate in aeronautical engineering from the Massachusetts Institute of Technology (MIT) and was a graduate of the Command and General Staff College and both the Army and the Navy War Colleges. Although he never flew a combat mission, MacDill was highly regarded for his innovative ideas regarding the development and advancement of the Army Air Corps. (Courtesy USF.)

Piloting an Army Air Corps North American BC-1 on the morning of November 9, 1938, Colonel MacDill crashed into the Anacostia section of Washington, DC, shortly after taking off from Bolling Field. MacDill, along with Pvt. Joseph G. Gloxner, was killed on impact. The cause of the crash was never determined. (Courtesy Library of Congress, Prints and Photographs Division, photograph by Harris and Ewing.)

At the time of his death, Colonel MacDill was serving on the War Department's General Staff in Washington, DC. MacDill was buried at Arlington National Cemetery on November 12, 1938. One year later, on November 30, 1939, Secretary of War Harry H. Woodring announced his decision to rename Tampa's Southeast Air Base in MacDill's honor. (Courtesy Library of Congress, Prints and Photographs Division, photograph by Harris and Ewing.)

As officer quarters and barracks were being constructed to house incoming troops in March 1940, soldiers who were not temporarily bivouacked at Tampa's Drew Field or quartered in old Port of Tampa customs and quarantine buildings established vast communities of pup tents that became popularly known as "Boom Town." Rain, snakes, dust, and clouds of mosquitoes made for trying conditions. (Courtesy 6 AMW/HO.)

In June 1940, the area of the peninsula that would later become the heart of MacDill Field was home to nothing more than alligators, snakes, dense palmetto scrub brush, and endless swaths of swampland. This picture highlights the tremendous effort that confronted the Works Progress Administration (WPA) workers who descended upon the field. Heavy machinery, of course, played a significant role. (Courtesy 6 AMW/HO.)

With measurements and surveys completed, clearing, grating, and paving operations for MacDill's future runways were well under way in June 1940. Of MacDill's estimated 5,700 acres of land, nearly 3,000 needed to be excavated by the WPA crews and quartermaster companies. By the completion date of the runways, 44,000 railroad cars of earth, scrub, and refuse had been removed from the field. (Courtesy 6 AMW/HO.)

Tampa mayor Robert E. Lee Chancey, enjoying a fine cigar, is flanked by Brigadier General Tinker (right), who assumed command of MacDill on May 17, 1940, and WDAE radio personality Sol Flieschman (in sunglasses). Chancey, who played a significant role in convincing the Army to select Tampa as the home of the Southeast Air Base, gives a speech on August 14, 1940, before the first load of concrete is poured for the runways. (Courtesy 6 AMW/HO.)

Brigadier General Tinker (second from right) and Tampa mayor Chancey (right) pose with MacDill Field resident engineers (left) and a representative from a construction firm at the runway ground-breaking ceremony. Until the runways could be completed, the bombers assigned to MacDill's 29th Bombardment Group were temporarily housed at Tampa's Drew Field, which until then had been nothing more than a small municipal field. (Courtesy 6 AMW/HO.)

Brigadier General Tinker and Mayor Chancey (center) pose with sharply dressed Tampa-area dignitaries, members of the Mayor's Commission, Hillsborough County commissioners, guests from the Greater Tampa Chamber of Commerce, members of the press, and representatives of the Portland Cement Company along a small portion of the runway that was about to be inundated by hundreds of tons of concrete. Watch out! (Courtesy 6 AMW/HO.)

WPA workers "lower the hammer" on the first load of concrete on the runway as excited troops and civilians look on. Paving was not limited to the runways, however, as WPA crews built 10 miles of curbing, 13 miles of storm sewers, and 8 miles of sanitary sewers. Tinker's primary concern, however, was undoubtedly getting the runways completed so he could have his bombers. (Courtesy 6 AMW/HO.)

Tons of steel were brought by railcar to MacDill through the Port of Tampa and used to reinforce the concrete to withstand the tonnage of bomb-laden B-17 Flying Fortresses scheduled to be assigned to the field. Five miles of barbed-wire fencing was also established around the field's perimeter prior to its opening. (Courtesy 6 AMW/HO.)

The scale of the project was enormous, and estimates placed the amount of concrete laid during the initial phases of MacDill's construction in the neighborhood of 2,650 cubic yards. A cubic yard of concrete equals an average of 2,600 pounds, or 1.3 tons, and measures 27 cubic feet. A conservative estimate would suggest over 3,400 tons of concrete were used, or roughly 6.9 million pounds. (Courtesy 6 AMW/HO.)

An aerial view of MacDill, captured on October 1, 1940, shows the partially completed officer quarters, club, and mess. Along the flight line, areas had been cleared where hangars were to be constructed, and large portions of the runways have been completed. Six miles of temporary roads had to be established during the construction period to accommodate the men and heavy machinery. (Courtesy 6 AMW/HO.)

Officers and enlisted men march in cadence along portions of MacDill's completed runways on November 19, 1940. Their firearms, perhaps, had not yet arrived, though extensive training with small arms, including .45-caliber pistols, Thompson submachine guns, Springfields, and Garands would become a regular part of a soldier's life on MacDill. (Courtesy HCPL.)

Men march in formation under the protective cover of B-17 Flying Fortresses in November 1940. Pilots taking off from Drew Field on July 15, 1940, completed the first bombing practice run on MacDill, dropping sandbag "bombs" on fixed ground targets set up by MacDill's engineers. Whether the bombardiers successfully struck their targets remains unknown. (Courtesy HCPL.)

Excavation operations continued in late 1940, as more infrastructure was required to support the growing number of troops. One such requirement included freshwater, and to support a base with a projected capacity of over 10,000 men, 12 miles of water lines were established across the field. Combined with the rain and vast swamplands, wet conditions abounded. (Courtesy 6 AMW/HO.)

By September 1940, a portion of the MacDill Field Station Hospital had been completed at the site of the modern-day base marina. Army surgeons assigned to the hospital would eventually perform every form of surgery except brain surgery. During the war, the hospital had its own X-ray department, physical therapy and orthopedic wards, pharmacy, and maternity department. Thankfully, modern anesthetics were available to the injured. (Courtesy 6 AMW/HO.)

By December 2, 1940, all five plots of land selected for use for MacDill's hangars had been surveyed and cleared and were under construction. Reinforced concrete aprons were also nearing completion. A subtle scene pictured here, the area of the hangar line would later become an energetic atmosphere as tool-wielding maintenance and ground crews, tanker trucks, armaments, and bombers danced to a carefully orchestrated symphony. During the war, MacDill Field was responsible for aircraft maintenance and repairs on all Army Air Corps assets stationed in the Gulf region, and eventually, two of MacDill's five hangars were devoted solely to meeting this obligation. The supervisor of maintenance, a position that eventually assumed the responsibilities of MacDill's maintenance subdepot, oversaw the hangars' men and equipment in the machine and sheet metal shops, engine exchange units, propeller and hydraulic shops, and painting and doping sections. Planes that had suffered so-called ground collisions were torn down. Undamaged and/or serviceable parts were removed and turned in to the Reclamation Section, with the remainder of the bird being turned over to the Salvage Section for disposal. (Courtesy 6 AMW/HO.)

The MacDill Field fire station, shown on December 2, 1940, had the dual purpose of serving as both the fire department and the headquarters for the guardsmen. The complex was maintained by Base Intelligence (S-2) along with the provost marshal, and base security functions were performed by the 851st and 1321st Guard Squadrons. The security force included fully armed MPs, sentry dogs, and civilian guards. Spotting towers were placed strategically around the base, vehicle inspections were performed on incoming and departing vehicles around vital areas, and speed limits of 25–35 miles per hour were strictly enforced. Civilian employees who held positions on the base were fingerprinted before being approved for a base pass. The post fire marshal's responsibilities included responding to crashes, fires, and other life-threatening emergencies and the operation, maintenance, and repair of all base fire protection equipment. These units were assisted by the 386th Signal Company (Aviation), which supervised emergency radio communications and switchboards. (Courtesy 6 AMW/HO.)

The first quadrant of officer quarters had been completed and subsequently occupied by December 2, 1940. For the unfortunate ones still housed in the humid and dusty Boom Town pup tents, the base by this time had at least engaged AAC engineer companies in larvicidal work to help eradicate the mosquito menace. These engineers were also responsible for the unsavory task of rodent and vermin control. (Courtesy 6 AMW/HO.)

Billeting for MacDill Field's high-ranking officers was under construction on January 1, 1941. These same buildings remain occupied today, continuing to serve as residences for MacDill's command-level staff and their families. MacDill's elementary school, located nearby, would later be named in Tinker's honor. (Courtesy 6 AMW/HO.)

Construction continued at the MacDill Field Station Hospital complex on January 1, 1941, as additional hospital wards were being created to handle the blossoming number of troops. During the war, American Red Cross volunteers, called "Gray Ladies," prepared surgical dressings, read to hospitalized soldiers, distributed stationery and reading materials, and aided soldiers in arranging emergency furloughs during family crises. (Courtesy 6 AMW/HO.)

MacDill Field runway construction continues on January 1, 1941; at the time, the base was less than two weeks from receiving its first bombers. AAC engineers would eventually assume the responsibilities of maintaining and repairing the field's heavily traveled runways and aprons. This picture puts in perspective the area of land that was required to be cleared by the WPA crews just to make room for the runways. (Courtesy 6 AMW/HO.)

Aqueduct systems can be seen under excavation along the runways on January 1, 1941. The systems kept the refined and natural gas, water, and sewage flowing to and from base storage tanks. Water pumping stations, water mains, and sewage pipes all needed to be laid and connected to the miles of water pipes, both for potable and non-potable water. (Courtesy 6 AMW/HO.)

A water tower is under construction on January 1, 1941, adjacent to the MacDill Field fire station and guardhouse. The crews who staffed the fire station undoubtedly played a heroic role when the Martin B-26 Marauders arrived. By late 1942, approximately 34 of MacDill's Marauders had experienced ground or water collisions, and the phrase "one a day in Tampa Bay" was born. (Courtesy 6 AMW/HO.)

This is an aerial view of MacDill Field from February 5, 1941. In January 1941, the 29th and 44th Bombardment Groups (Heavy) combined with the 13 Bombardment Group (Medium) to form the 3rd Bombardment Wing on MacDill, commanded by Brigadier General Tinker. The headquarters squadron of the 3rd Bombardment Wing later became the headquarters section of the 3rd Bomber Command when it was activated on MacDill under the Third Air Force on August 13, 1941. The

Third Air Force, which was one of America's first four numbered air forces, was originally established as the Southeast Air District on October 19, 1940, and was activated on MacDill on December 18, 1940. The 3rd Bomber Command, under Gen. Follett Bradley, assumed the responsibility for all heavy bombardment fields under the Third Air Force. (Courtesy 6 AMW/HO.)

The Drew Field Bomb Group Camp, which would later become Tampa International Airport, is seen in November 11, 1940, as little more than a minimally equipped municipal airfield. Men and planes of the 29th Bombardment Group were encamped at Drew Field until MacDill's runways were ready to receive flights. Douglas B-18 Bolos and Northrop A-17 Nomad bombers can be seen on the field. (Courtesy 6 AMW/HO.)

The bombers and men of the 29th Bombardment Group remained at Drew Field, in conditions not much better than those available on MacDill, until the historic day of January 14, 1941, when Brigadier General Tinker, piloting a Douglas B-18 Bolo from Drew, landed the first bomber on MacDill. MacDill Field was open for business. (Courtesy 6 AMW/HO.)

Survey work continued on MacDill during the summer of 1941. The engineer companies, partly responsible for this work, included officers and enlisted men, civilians, and skilled and unskilled laborers. Many of the civilians were either hired from the civil service register or hired locally and given war service appointments. Trained to operate and maintain heavy equipment and road-building machinery, MacDill's combat engineers also included demolition and weapons specialists, diesel mechanics, well drillers, camouflage technicians, radio operators, and machinists. Expanded programs included training in the use of the bazooka, chemical warfare agents, and the laying and defusing of mines. When a break was needed, the men could lay in the shade and enjoy the latest issue of MacDill's first newspaper, the *Flyleaf*, which debuted on April 18, 1941, and was published every Saturday by the base Public Relations Office. (Courtesy 6 AMW/HO.)

The engineering officers and men were responsible for infrastructure construction and maintenance, providing adequate housing, and maintaining the water and sewage facilities, drainage systems, roads, runways, and hangars. The machete was undoubtedly a popular tool of choice during MacDill's early days. (Courtesy 6 AMW/HO.)

The civilians within the engineering companies also served in clerical and administrative fields and as aircraft and instrument mechanics, leather and canvas workers, painters, sheet metal workers, welders, woodworkers, blacksmiths, carpenters, and electricians. It is unclear if they were forewarned that their duties would likely include wading through waist-deep muck. (Courtesy 6 AMW/HO.)

Under the base beautification program, lovely copses of pine, palm, and banana trees were maintained for the pleasure of the troops. Palmetto scrub brush, however, was the real enemy during the summer of 1941, as these men can be seen working so diligently towards their eradication—a difficult job, for sure. (Courtesy 6 AMW/HO.)

While these men were plowing through lands on MacDill, the Nazis and European Axis powers were engaged in a similar activity, albeit at the expense of lives rather than foliage. By the summer of 1941, when this picture was taken, the Axis powers had captured Poland, Denmark, Norway, France, and Belgium, to name a few, and Operation Barbarossa, the invasion of the Soviet Union, had just commenced. (Courtesy 6 AMW/HO.)

Enjoying a cigarette, a civilian mired in muck holds a pose while performing surveys during the summer of 1941. Beginning in 1943, men like this began receiving help from Tampa-area women, who were brought on base to fill positions including riveting, welding, fabric doping, sheet metal work, and parachute rigging. (Courtesy 6 AMW/HO.)

By the summer of 1941, four miles of gas lines, required for the thousands of gallons that would be needed to quench the appetite of the thirsty bombers, were laid. Trucks and heavy machinery can be seen sharing the load. (Courtesy 6 AMW/HO.)

During the initial phases of MacDill's construction, eight miles of underground telephone conduit were laid (shown here during the summer of 1941), and maintenance of them would become the responsibility of the Signal Corps. Notably, the Air Corps was actually an outgrowth of the Signal Corps here in America—before planes were powerful enough to wield ordnance, their primary purpose was ferrying message traffic. (Courtesy 6 AMW/HO.)

A worker walks precariously along the middle section of water-filled ditches. Wells and storm drainage systems were also excavated during the summer of 1941. To the left is an old shack. The southern area of MacDill, previously known as Gadsden's Point, had a few families of settlers when the War Department purchased the land. (Courtesy 6 AMW/HO.)

During the summer of 1941, MacDill's Burma Road was under construction and eventually became a one-and-a-quarter-mile obstacle course used to train the drivers of Jeeps and so-called deuce-and-a-half personnel carriers (which weighed two and a half tons) for the wartime conditions that would be found on the front. The grueling course led drivers through a small lake, ditches, flooded palmetto scrubs, stumps, thick brush, loose sand, ravines, and a morass of deep mud, which at times reached over the hood. When traction failed, the drivers leapt into the muck and were required to winch themselves free by attaching a cable to a tree. Or worse, it was a long and solemn walk back to the base motor pool, where the soldier would be guaranteed to be heckled and on the losing end of a good tongue lashing from an angry desk sergeant. (Courtesy 6 AMW/HO.)

Barracks for enlisted personnel were under construction during the summer of 1941. The mundane life of the early occupants of barracks, like the one shown, would soon change for the better as the new Post Exchange (PX) was under development. MacDill's first PX was a meager counter located on the first floor of one of the early two-story enlisted men's barracks. (Courtesy 6 AMW/HO.)

The new Post Exchange (PX) blossomed into a bustling enterprise, including the Wingspread Soda Bar (a favorite spot for a scoop of ice cream), the enlisted men's cafeteria, a Beer Bar, and the merchandise store, which sold shoes, clothing, and the two staples required by every soldier: coffee and tobacco. The cafeteria was open 24 hours; unfortunately, the Beer Bar was not. (Courtesy 6 AMW/HO.)

Barracks construction continued during the summer of 1941. To provide for the troops, the new PX was located adjacent to the base headquarters, theater, and gymnasium, and it included two outdoor patios with umbrellas, shaded tables, and a soda garden and beer garden. The complex also included a meat market, service station, and a cafeteria for MacDill's civilian employees. (Courtesy 6 AMW/HO.)

The PX boasted nine barber shops employing 50 barbers, a shoe repair and tailor shop, and dry cleaning and pressing shops. Sub-exchanges were dispersed around various areas of MacDill for the convenience of the troops, including at the hospital, the so-called casual camp, and along the hangar line. A fleet of four trucks ferried supplies between the PX warehouse and the various locations. (Courtesy 6 AMW/HO.)

Rail lines were laid throughout MacDill, as can be seen in some of the preceding pictures, and connected the growing base with the Port of Tampa. By the summer of 1941, daily trips between the port and MacDill were regularly scheduled, hauling out waste and debris and bringing in 150–200 carloads of supplies a month. (Courtesy 6 AMW/HO.)

Construction began on Hangar No. 5 during the summer of 1941, while other hangars were nearing completion. In addition to the hangars and other infrastructure, 29 miles of overhead electrical wiring were strung in conjunction with an electrical metering station being constructed to keep electricity flowing throughout MacDill. A lonely bomber can be seen along the hangar line. (Courtesy 6 AMW/HO.)

As German Messerschmitts were launching Blitzkrieg raids into the skies over European Allied nations and engaging RAF fighters in the Battle of Britain, this was not the comforting vision of America's response to airpower one might expect, though biplane trainers were a regular fixture in MacDill's earliest days. Parked along an unfinished portion of MacDill's apron, this trainer appears anything but lethal. (Courtesy USF.)

Men relax outside a MacDill hangar that was under construction during the summer of 1941. Unable to communicate by cell phones and text messages, men gathered in person to hear the latest "poop and scuttlebutt." Notably, the base Signal Corps was still utilizing homing pigeons—at the time, considered one of the most reliable methods of communication, as they made difficult targets for enemy marksmen. (Courtesy 6 AMW/HO.)

Men in overalls are seen studying schematics as a hangar in the background is nearing completion on June 3, 1941. Note the men on the roof constructing a small control terminal. The completed base water tower can be seen over the hangar's right shoulder, and fuel trucks are arranged along the apron, ready to disperse their contents. No smoking! (Courtesy HCPL.)

Brigadier General Tinker is seen leading a salute on MacDill Field about 1941. Later reassigned to Hawaii on July 16, 1941, Tinker was killed in action piloting a Liberator during the Battle of Midway on June 7, 1942. By then promoted to major general, at the time the highest rank ever achieved by a Native American in the US Army, Tinker became the first Air Corps general to be killed during World War II. (Courtesy HCPL.)

Brigadier General Tinker (second from left) and his staff pose in front of Tinker's plane with Maj. Gen. Barton Kyle Yount (far left) about 1941. In 1940, Yount took command of the Southeast Air District, headquartered in Tampa, which later became the Third Air Force. Yount routinely visited MacDill to confer with Tinker about their area of responsibility in and around Florida, including patrolling the waters for enemy submarines, or U-boats. As a result of America's Lend-Lease Act, in which armaments and munitions were supplied to struggling Allied nations, Nazi Germany initiated a terror campaign on the open seas on transports sailing from US and Canadian waters to Europe. (Courtesy 6 AMW/HO.)

Brigadier General Tinker (center) poses with his men and a delegation from the air vice-marshal's staff of the British Royal Air Force (RAF), who came to inspect the new field about 1941. This marked MacDill's first visit from a delegation of foreign military representatives. RAF personnel trained at both Drane Field (in Lakeland, Florida) and Avon Park Air Base, Florida, during World War II. (Courtesy 6 AMW/HO.)

Brigadier General Tinker and one of his staff members chat with visiting RAF personnel and a local woman about 1941. On July 16, 1941, Tinker was transferred to Hawaii, and his executive officer, Col. Harry H. Young, succeeded him as MacDill's commander. The RAF trained in Florida under the Lodwick School of Aeronautics, a civilian flight school contracted by the US War Department. (Courtesy 6 AMW/HO.)

Named after Brig. Gen. William "Billy" Mitchell, the USS *General William Mitchell* arrived at MacDill in 1941 and served as a personal transport craft for General Tinker. The ship served a secondary mission as a crash rescue boat for downed flyers in Hillsborough Bay or the Gulf of Mexico. During the war, the seamen kept their eyes peeled for German U-boats trying to infiltrate the surrounding waters. (Courtesy 6 AMW/HO.)

The *Mitchell* was the first of many boats to arrive, making up what would later be referred to as "MacDill's Navy" about 1941. Operated by MacDill Field's Quartermaster Boat Company, the organization also maintained an 83-foot salvage vessel outfitted with diving equipment for performing salvage work on downed bombers. (Courtesy 6 AMW/HO.)

Pictured is the MacDill Field Enlisted Men's Beach Club about 1941. When not enjoying the beaches along MacDill's shore lines, troops could visit the Enlisted Men's Service Club (which opened to great fanfare on October 11, 1941) and toss a nickel into a wishing well that collected donations for the Army Air Forces Aid Society. (Courtesy USF.)

The MacDill Field Beach Club is pictured about 1941. Off-base activities abounded during the war as well, and soldiers enjoyed sailing in St. Petersburg, visiting the Gulf beaches, sipping drinks at the Colonnade on Bayshore Boulevard, visiting the University of Tampa's library and museum attractions, skating at the Davis Island Coliseum, and frequenting various Tampa-area USO clubs. (Courtesy USF.)

On April 16, 1941, the base received its formal dedication and was opened to the public for the ceremony. Residents were allowed to dine in the MacDill mess halls, and for 50¢, they enjoyed a full "square," with selections including split-pea soup with oyster crackers, Swiss steak, fried ham with barbecue sauce, and a choice variety of vegetables: sweet pickles, sliced tomatoes, candied yams, boiled kidney beans, and buttered spinach, to name a few. MacDill's widow and her two daughters were the honored guests. (Courtesy 6 AMW/HO.)

The principal speaker was Brig. Gen. Herbert A. Dargue, the official representative to the chief of the Air Corps and the War Department. Claude D. Pepper, Florida's "Fighting Senator," also gave a profound speech, saying, "America is today the only hope of the democracies, and perhaps in six months, or less, the strong arm of the United States may be their only protection. America will not fail; it will not permit civilization to be destroyed by a beast already preparing for the kill." (Courtesy of the author.)

The nearly completed MacDill Field Station Hospital is shown on December 5, 1941. Also on this day, MacDill-based soldiers performed a mock invasion of MacDill from the Interbay Peninsula. MacDill was said to have acquitted itself well. With this being two days prior to the Japanese bombing of Pearl Harbor, a completed hospital and soldiers experienced in amphibious landings could not have come at a more opportune time. (Courtesy 6 AMW/HO.)

Deceptive camouflage officers and men known as camoufleurs are shown manufacturing a dummy plane about 1941. The camoufleurs, assisted by base engineers, constructed dummy tanks, planes, and antiaircraft batteries out of wood and chicken wire. Collapsible bushes concealed machine gun nests, and camouflaged lookout nests lined the beaches because of the real and persistent threat posed by Nazi U-boats and possible Japanese fighters or sapper units. (Courtesy 6 AMW/HO.)

Douglas A-20A Havoc bombers fly in formation over two of MacDill's hangars about 1941. Over 1,000 of these light bombers were supplied to the British RAF through the Lend-Lease Act, and the British nicknamed them "Boston." The Havoc/Boston was a mainstay for the US, British, and Soviet air forces and saw significant action in virtually every theater of the war. (*Tampa Tribune* file photograph used with their permission.)

108—Barracks at Mac Dill Field, U. S. Army Air Base, Tampa, Fla.

This postcard from 1941 depicts a Douglas B-18 Bolo flying solo over MacDill barracks. Bolo formations parked in tight groupings for security purposes were a favorite target for Japanese fighter squadrons during the raid on Pearl Harbor on December 7, 1941. By 1942, the United States began replacing the medium bomber with airframes deemed more combat effective. (Courtesy author.)

Two

GLOBAL CONFLAGRATION

During World War II, the number of personnel assigned to MacDill Field swelled from 600 to over 10,000, and estimates place the number of combat crews trained on the base at over 50,000. MacDill's 29th and 44th Bombardment Groups were among the first of America's Army Air Corps to be sent into battle. Soldiers arrived at MacDill's Operational Training Units (OTUs) straight out of basic training, and during the war, there were several thousand men training at any given time, pouring through the program at six-week intervals. After the initial six-week program concluded, the trainees would graduate into MacDill combat units and spend another six weeks sharpening their skills before being sent to the front. Courses included training for pilots, bombardiers, navigators, aerial gunners, radio operators, armament and ordnance technicians, aircraft and engine mechanics, and even cooks and bakers. At peak, an entire hangar was devoted to the OTU program; it was divided and arranged into classrooms, which included static displays of aircraft engines, electric propellers, radio compartments, and ordnance and weaponry. And in helping to shoulder one of the burdens of victory, MacDill eventually detained several hundred German prisoners of war (POWs) during 1944 and 1945.

Paul W. Tibbets Jr., seemingly just another anonymous soul yearning to serve his country, arrived on MacDill in February 1942 and reported for duty to the 29th Bombardment Group as an engineering officer. From February 1942 to June 1942, Tibbets was a B-17 Flying Fortress pilot-in-training on MacDill. Tibbets deployed to England in June 1942 and participated in the first B-17 Flying Fortress bombing raid against occupied Europe. Tibbets later piloted the B-29 Superfortress *Enola Gay*, named after his mother, in America's first atomic bomb mission, dropping the five-ton "Little Boy" on Hiroshima on August 6, 1945. His skills were mastered on MacDill Field and in the skies over Tampa and the Mullet Key Gunnery Range.

A postcard from 1941 depicts Douglas B-18 Bolos flying in formation over the city of Tampa, with Davis Island and Hillsborough Bay visible in the background. Outclassed and obsolete by the time America entered World War II, the B-18s did not serve a substantial role during the war, being replaced by the B-17 Flying Fortress and B-26 Marauder, to name a few. (Courtesy author.)

This postcard from 1941 shows soldiers peeling potatoes among the pup tents of the infamous Boom Town, located at the "corner of Sand Avenue and Dust Boulevard." When not using sharpened implements against vegetables, soldiers could participate in the MacDill Field Military Police bayonet course, which included nine swinging dummies for issuing "thrusts, parries, jabs and butt strokes" to learn the "delivery of cold steel." (Courtesy author.)

MacDill airmen stand in front of a Boeing B-17 Flying Fortress about 1941. Referred to as "battleships of the air," the B-17s were arguably the most formidable bombers of the war. The bomber bristled with .50-caliber machine guns from its nose, tail, sides, belly, and back and was capable of devastating high-altitude precision bombing, including daylight raids over enemy-occupied territory. (Courtesy 6 AMW/HO.)

MacDill Field–based B-17s fly in formation over Florida about 1942. Flying Fortresses often blotted out the skies over enemy territory, flying in massive 1,000-plus-plane armadas. Part of the training on MacDill included teaching the pilots how to take evasive actions from flak (anti-aircraft artillery—Triple A or AAA), including when to turn into the 88-milimeter airbursts and when to turn away from them. (Courtesy TBHC.)

The first B-26 Marauder arrived on MacDill on June 1, 1942. The Marauders enjoyed the lowest loss rate of any Allied bomber during the war, and over half of the combat groups who piloted the B-26 were trained on MacDill. The bomber's short, "clipped" wings, however, made for dangerous training. Pilots were required to make landings while traveling near 130 miles per hour and struggled with the bomber's sensitive, temperamental flight characteristics. (Courtesy USF.)

A 1941 MacDill Field–issued information booklet depicts a B-26 Marauder and touts MacDill as the "Southeast's largest heavy bombardment air base." The Marauder combat crews were composed of six men: a pilot, copilot, radio operator, aerial engineer, armorer-gunner, and bombardier-navigator. The Marauders included two 2,000-horsepower engines, and pilots were required to graduate from hundreds of hours of training on MacDill. (Courtesy author.)

One of the oldest units on MacDill was the 3rd Photographic Mapping Squadron of the 1st Mapping Group, which arrived on December 21, 1941. The squadron boasted one of the finest photographic labs in the country. Its compound consisted of five large buildings, and at capacity, it was capable of developing 25,000 prints a day. Some of its photographs were undoubtedly used for this 1940s postcard. (Courtesy author.)

Most likely a compilation of both MacDill and Drew Field war birds, this 1940s postcard depicts the aerial firepower available to the United States during the war. Staffed with highly skilled photographic technicians, the 3rd Photographic Mapping Squadron's first assignment included charting the Western hemisphere from the air, the purpose of which was to secure accurate maps and aerial photographs to define terrain and pinpoint enemy targets. (Courtesy author.)

Pictured is a "MacDill Navy" crash boat about 1943. MacDill Field's Quartermaster Boat Company, which maintained the so-called navy, was on duty around the clock and notified immediately during a crash or forced water landing, deploying within minutes of the call. These "soldier-sailors" were trained in lifesaving techniques and seamanship, including knot tying, rope splicing, and nautical navigation methodology. (Courtesy 6 AMW/HO.)

MacDill Navy crash boat crewmen are pictured about 1943 in front of what were referred to as J-boats—high-powered speedboats that carried basic medical equipment and could quickly respond to maritime emergencies. Larger hospital ships, staffed with medical officers and equipped with dispensaries, were kept on standby 24 hours a day, along with larger crash boats. (Courtesy 6 AMW/HO.)

Pictured is the MacDill Field Navy shipyard, home of MacDill's Quartermaster Boat Company in about 1943. The *General Tinker* ferryboat was docked here, as well as the J-boats and hospital ships. A second, smaller dock (which would later become MacDill's marina) was located near the base hospital. The soldier-sailors were not completely benign, as they were also trained marksmen, equipped to eliminate any maritime threats. (Courtesy 6 AMW/HO.)

A large crash boat, shown in the early 1940s, trawls the waters of Hillsborough Bay, ready to respond to a crash or nautical emergency. The Quartermaster Boat Company also maintained small, flat-bottom "swamp gliders," which were propelled by an aircraft engine that enabled them to skim across the surface for shallow-water rescues (no doubt an early ancestor to the modern airboats). (Courtesy 6 AMW/HO.)

A highly animated Sgt. Robert R. Stubbs (right) explains to a somewhat skeptical-looking Capt. Jean Fogle the intricacies of his invention, a new form of fragmentation bomb. Stubbs had been working on the bomb for three years and came to MacDill Field on April 2, 1942, to see it tested. Judging from his enthusiastic appearance, the results of the test must have been terrific. Forward-thinking Americans like Stubbs put their minds to task and developed several innovative munitions for destroying large swaths of enemy-held territory, particularly the incendiaries, which, as the reader likely recalls, wiped out more of Japan than the combined results of the atomic bombs dropped on Hiroshima and Nagasaki. (Courtesy author.)

MacDill's chemical warfare units, known as the "gas troops," were highly specialized and trained in the deployment of "test tube death." The units were attached to the Army Air Corps and were charged with the storage and care of chemical warfare materials. In the 1940s, each of MacDill's bomb wings had a chemical warfare officer who supervised both the offensive and defensive chemical warfare activities. (Courtesy 6 AMW/HO.)

Chemical warfare agents were viewed as a favorable method for neutralizing large numbers of enemy forces, though they were also used to produce robust volumes of smoke for screening operations and as incendiaries to produce large swaths of destructive fires. MacDill's gas troops trained base personnel to defend themselves from chemical attacks, supervised the distribution of gas masks, and performed gas reconnaissance missions. (Courtesy 6 AMW/HO.)

Members of the Women's Army Auxiliary Corps (WAACs), later redesignated Women's Army Corps (WACs), are seen arriving at MacDill on April 27, 1943. The WAACs received four weeks of basic training in Daytona Beach, Florida, which included military customs and regulations, sanitation and hygiene, close order drill, physical training, and defense against chemical and air attacks. Tampa residents banded together to donate irons for the ladies (ironing boards came standard with the rooms). The 653rd WAAC Photo Laboratory Company, using the 3rd Mapping Squadron's facilities, went through 12,000 gallons of chemicals per month operating the lab's massive rotary washers and dryers and was responsible for finishing, developing, and drying rolls of aerial film and processing, inspecting, and interpreting as many as 1,000 photographs per hour. The WAACs' photographs and charts were deployed to every theater of war. (Courtesy 6 AMW/HO.)

The **CARRYALL**

VOL. 2 NO. 8 ENGINEER AVIATION UNIT TRAINING CENTER, MACDILL FIELD, FLA. AUG. 1944

The *Carryall* (the August 1944 edition is pictured here) was the magazine of MacDill's 3rd Engineer Aviation Unit Training Center (EAUTC), an outgrowth of the 927th Engineer Aviation Regiment, an all–African American unit that was activated on MacDill on March 18, 1943. At the publishing of this edition, 65,000 copies of the magazine had rolled of the press in its brief, 10-month duration. At the time, the *Carryall* was the only publication of its kind in the United States completely staffed and run by African American personnel. Pictured on the cover is Brig. Gen. Benjamin O. Davis Sr., the first African American general officer in the US Army and at the time a special assistant to the Army's inspector general. Davis was awarded both the Bronze Star and the Distinguished Service Medals for his meritorious service during the war. Davis's son Benjamin O. Davis Jr., leader of the famed Tuskegee Airmen, was the fourth African American to graduate from the US Military Academy and the first African American to achieve the rank of general officer in the US Air Force. (Courtesy author.)

Military personnel and civilians of MacDill Field's Quartermaster Corps pose together in the 1940s. The Quartermaster Corps supplied every stitch of clothing and apparel from its general supply warehouse, and its purchasing and contracting office had the responsibility of purchasing, procuring, storing, and distributing shoes, helmets, and office stationery and equipment. The subsistence division had dry and cold storage facilities for food and perishables. (Courtesy TBHC.)

MacDill Field Quartermaster Corps celebrates a Christmas party together about 1944. Known as one of the finest bases in the country, as the war progressed, MacDill underwent large expansion and beautification projects. The field boasted an Enlisted Men's Service Club, Officer's Club, Post Exchange, soda fountain, gymnasium, bowling alley, squadron day rooms, and a hospital boasting complete medical and surgical services. (Courtesy TBHC.)

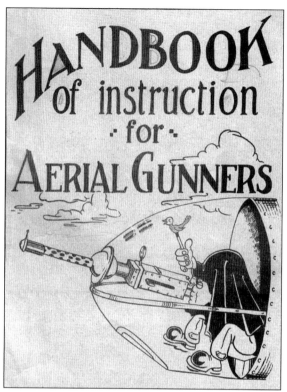

In this MacDill-produced *Handbook of Instruction for Aerial Gunners* from the 1940s, gunners were instructed in "applying all the scientific formulas of death." *Thunderbird*, another MacDill publication, debuted on February 1, 1943. Known as the "Fighting Man's Magazine" or the "Mirror of MacDill," the *Thunderbird* was the "Official MacDill Field Quarterly" and intended to record MacDill's "flaming pages of history." (Courtesy author.)

A trainee is shown engaged in turret practice with the "venomous muzzles" of "twin fifties" in the 1940s. OTU classrooms included batteries of static waist guns as well as chin, top, and ball turrets located in hangar bays, some of which were suspended from hangar platforms to simulate their various positions on the Flying Fortresses and Marauders. (Courtesy 6 AMW/HO.)

Beginning with classroom training, aerial gunnery students learned ballistics, maintenance, sighting techniques, and aircraft recognition and studied turrets and flex guns in the armament section until these aspects were second nature to them, and they became very proficient in their business of killing. Students were required to learn to disassemble and reassemble the .50-calibers while wearing heavy gloves, simulating the freezing conditions they would encounter at high altitudes over enemy-held territory. Armament specialists became so accustomed with their wares that they were able to dismantle and reassemble machine guns while blindfolded. In the image, gunnery training occurs at the ball turret (top left); turret gunnery practice takes place on the skeet range (top right); a gunner trains in tracking and intercepting an enemy fighter (middle left); a section of the turret gunnery department appears (middle right); troops are trained in the operation of the flexible waist gun (bottom left); and prospective tail gunners are being introduced to their new weapon (bottom right). (Courtesy 6 AMW/HO.)

A waist gunner is shown firing a machine gun in the 1940s. Airborne training included firing a "camera gun" at friendly pursuit aircraft simulating enemy fighters, with accuracy later verified through developed film. Students also used live .50-calibers to hose down water targets placed in the Gulf of Mexico. Targets were also towed by B-26 tow target detachments, allowing students to fire at airborne targets. (Courtesy 6 AMW/HO.)

Tiny aircraft replicas were mounted on mechanical pulley systems to simulate enemy fighters, allowing students to study sighting techniques as the replicas completed rotational arcs. The targets revolved slowly until the gunner achieved a level of acquaintance, then the revolutions sped up so the trainee could master lead times. Gunners also sat behind mounted .50-calibers with a motion picture projector beaming a light onto a screen. (Courtesy 6 AMW/HO.)

MacDill's personnel within the Ordnance Department included specialists trained in research and development, ordnance specifications, fire control systems, the storage and distribution of explosives, and loading bomb and machine gun magazines. Their responsibilities included equipping and supplying the men and bombers with ammunition and armaments, training and issuing small arms and grenades to base personnel, and delivering the ordnance to the awaiting bombers. (Courtesy 6 AMW/HO.)

Shown is a portion of the shotgun range, which included real and mock waist-gun positions and turrets, raised off the ground on wooden or aircraft platforms. Shotguns replaced the .50-calibers in the turrets or were mounted alongside the waist gun positions, and students blasted away at clay pigeons sailing through the air in simulation of enemy Messerschmitts and Zeros. (Courtesy 6 AMW/HO.)

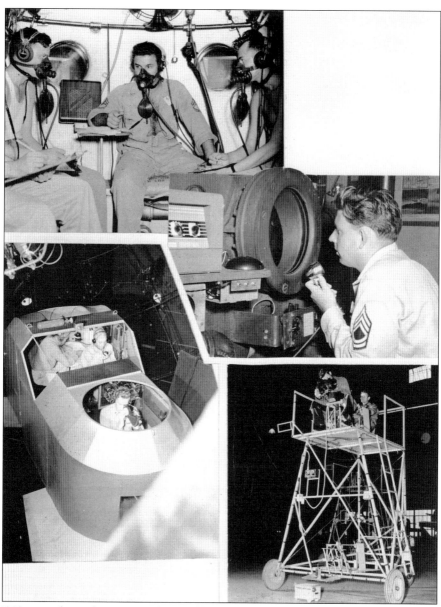

This 1940s view shows the interior of MacDill's altitude chamber (top left), its effects being closely monitored (center right), the celestial navigation trainer (bottom left), and a bombardier bombing mock targets from his high chair (bottom right). Sitting in the high chairs, future bombardiers trained their bombsites on simulated miniature targets arranged on the hangars' floors. The seats would be raised and lowered over the mock targets so bombardiers could hone the skills that would be required for low- and high-level bombing runs. The Link Celestial Navigation Trainer encapsulated a student in an enclosed silo under a canopy that projected lights in simulation of constellations. The dome revolved to simulate changes in the plane's position. This allowed the trainees to study night celestial flying using a sextant. For daylight training, the Link projected moving video images of terrain below the fuselage, providing a sensation of flight. While studying the constellations and terrain, the student received instructions and guidance via radio messages from an instructor. (Courtesy 6 AMW/HO.)

A bombardier is engaged in target training about 1944. When not engaged in dropping lethal loads, the bombardiers, or "ambassadors of death," served as navigators, taking radio compass readings and following enemy frequencies to their point of origin. The bombardiers assumed control of the bomber during the final approach, and to stay on target, pilots were required to cease all evasive action. (Courtesy 6 AMW/HO.)

MacDill bombardier trainees are seen in their high chairs in the 1940s. The OTU and RTU navigation courses taught bombardiers dead reckoning procedures (use of instruments to calculate time, speed, and distance with wind and pressure) and the use of a radio compass. Instruments recorded the student's progress on navigational charts, which were later used to study the precision of his calculations. (Courtesy 6 AMW/HO.)

A navigator is seen shooting the octant in the 1940s. OTU and RTU students learned calculation methods of the altimeter, air speed indicator, and driftmeter and were introduced to the C-1 automatic pilot, which synchronized with the bomb site to allow the bombardier full control of the aircraft. The study of bomb theory included the various effects of different munitions. (Courtesy 6 AMW/HO.)

115—Island Target Range for Mac Dill Field Bombers at Tampa, Fla.

The "Island target range for MacDill Field bombers" noted on this 1940s postcard refers to Mullet Key, which had previously been nothing more than a tranquil bird sanctuary. Pounded during the war, Mullet Key was where trainees learned the deployment and effects of their "death-dealing mechanisms." Ferried back and forth by MacDill's Quartermaster Boat Company, MacDill engineering units maintained Mullet Key's targets and ranges and tabulated a pilot's score from his bombing and strafing runs. (Courtesy author.)

116—Loading Bombs on Flying Fortress　　　Fla.

PHOTOGRAPH BY ARMY AIR CORPS

Ordnance personnel are seen loading bombs on a Flying Fortress in this 1940s postcard. MacDill's hangar line was a hurried scene during the war, with ordnance personnel zipping around to deliver the bombs and load .50-caliber shells in the magazine area. Cranes were used to jack the bombs into the belly of the bomber. (Courtesy author.)

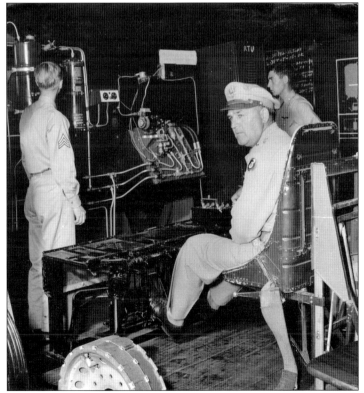

Brig. Gen. James E. Parker, shown inspecting a hydraulic system, assumed the lead of 3rd Bomber Command on MacDill on November 4, 1942. Besides training the pilots and crew of bombers, part of the responsibility of the 3rd Bomber Command included patrolling the surrounding waters by air for enemy submarines. (Courtesy 6 AMW/HO.)

Brig. Gen. James E. Parker (left), of 3rd Bomber Command, is seen inspecting a turret tracking system in the 1940s. During his tenure, it was part of Parker's responsibilities to make sure all crewmen who served aboard a bomber were combat-ready gunners, qualified through the completion of an extensive gunnery training program. (Courtesy 6 AMW/HO.)

MacDill Field Station Hospital medical officers attend the 3rd Bomber Command Unit Surgeons' Conference on MacDill Field on June 23, 1944. The hospital was staffed with doctors, surgeons, dentists, and nurses and boasted the finest equipment in the Army. The base dispensary was a branch of the hospital and distributed preventative medicines, including the then-new penicillin. (Courtesy 6 AMW/HO.)

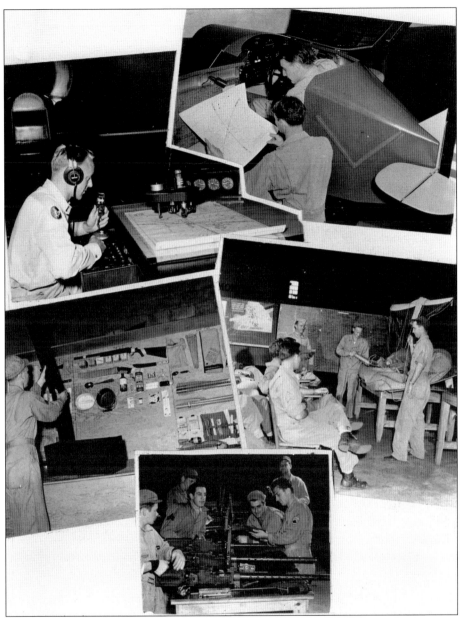

A trainee can be seen using a Link trainer (top right), with his progress being closely monitored (left). Also visible are the contents of a life raft (lower left), an instructor demonstrating the proper use of a life raft (right), and soldiers receiving machine gun instructions (bottom). When trainees were not engaged in constructive activities, they could enjoy a free round-trip ride aboard the *General Clarence L. Tinker* ferryboat in their Class Bs to sip (or guzzle) cold brews in Ybor City. Free-time favorites also included weekly open-air concerts and dances at the Service Club; playing baseball, basketball, and handball; honing one's skills at the archery range; or pumping iron at one of MacDill's three large gyms. Maintained by the Special Services Branch, the Enlisted Men's Service Club featured a dance floor, day rooms, a game room with pool, ping-pong, and card tables, reading rooms, and a soda bar and cafeteria. Meeting and romancing a pretty WAC at the outdoor dance pavilion was certainly a favorite as well. (Courtesy 6 AMW/HO.)

Men are seen performing routine maintenance on the engine of a B-17 Flying Fortress in the 1940s. The engines received regular 100-hour check-ups, and all B-17s were completely overhauled after every 500 hours of flight time. Electrical specialists were required to memorize the miles of wiring that lined each bomber and to troubleshoot quickly if any problems arose. (Courtesy 6 AMW/HO.)

MacDill's Supervisor of Supply was responsible for supplying all organizations stationed on MacDill and MacDill's subfields. The organization was comprised of six departments, including Quartermaster Supply Officer, Ordnance Officer, Signal Property Officer, Engineer Property Officer, Chemical Property Officer, and Air Corps Supply Officer. Known informally as the housekeeping section, this department made sure the aircraft mechanics had all the right tools and parts. (Courtesy 6 AMW/HO.)

These gentlemen—some interested and some apparently not—sit in chairs labeled "3rd B.C." (Bomber Command) while participating in an OTU engine maintenance course in the 1940s. Some of these men may have been antsy for the Saturday night fights. Provided by the base Special Services Branch, MacDill's favorite pastime was boxing, which drew capacity crowds of over 3,000 to the gym to watch every card. (Courtesy 6 AMW/HO.)

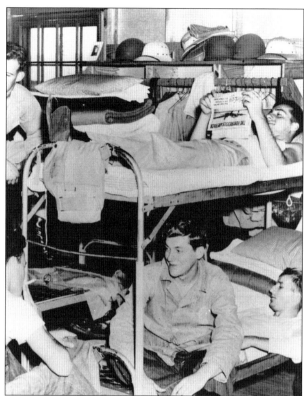

Soldiers, one of whom can be seen reading a newspaper proclaiming "The Fortresses are Back," lounge in their barracks about 1943. When not training, these men could enjoy a quiet afternoon reading one of the post library's 10,000 volumes, lounge on one of the PX open-air patios, or enjoy some tunes at the MacDill Bandshell, which held its first concert on July 3, 1943. (Courtesy 6 AMW/HO.)

Shown is a 1940s postcard depicting the MacDill Field Officers' Club. Manuel Garcia, better known as "MacDill Manny," was the host of the club, which was known as one of the finest. The club included a large room for hosting dinner parties, an air-conditioned bar, a game room, and a modern kitchen with expert chefs and cooks on site. (Courtesy author.)

Pictured in this 1940s postcard is the MacDill Field Base Hospital. Film star Lily Damita (by then divorced from Errol Flynn) visited the hospital during the war, one of many celebrities who stopped in to see the troops. Model planes were hung from the ceilings in the convalescent training program to teach wounded troops aircraft identification. The convalescent program included, of all things, boxing. (Courtesy author.)

MacDill's post laundry, opened June 16, 1943, was a one-acre facility that included three 3,500-gallon water tanks, a warehouse, and a powerplant with three 200-horsepower burners. Employing 310 workers—230 of them women—operating on two shifts, the $1 million facility handled approximately 525,000 pieces of laundry a week, 375,000 of which were enlisted uniforms—mattress covers, sheets, and pillow cases made up the rest. (Courtesy 6 AMW/HO.)

93—U. S. Bombers from Mac Dill Field Army Base over Lafayette Street Bridge, Tampa, Fla.

A 1940s postcard depicts B-17 Flying Fortresses flying in formation near downtown Tampa as life carries on as usual on the Lafayette Street Bridge. The minarets of the University of Tampa can be seen in the background. To clarify, it can be assumed that these bombers were not targeting Tampa civilians. (Courtesy author.)

Aerial View of MacDill Field, Army Air Base, Tampa, Florida

TAMPA SKYLINE

PETER O. KNIGHT AIRPORT

B-17s are seen at altitude over MacDill in this 1940s postcard. As of 1944, medium and heavy bombers were carrying and deploying bombs weighing anywhere from 17 to 4,000 pounds, costing between $25 and $5,000 each. The bombers were armed with .30- and .50-caliber machine guns capable of firing 1,000 rounds per minute and carried 20-millimeter and 37-millimeter canons. (Courtesy author.)

A less-than-enthusiastic MacDill airman displays his "Mae West" life vest on Drew Field in the 1940s. When the boys from the Quartermaster Boat Company were dithering, downed pilots could rely on these vests to keep them afloat until help arrived. The waterlogged men could then rely on the post laundry's batteries of Ellis driers and steam pressers to make their uniforms whole again. (Courtesy 6 AMW/HO.)

MacDill Field pilots and crewmen train for water landings on a man-made lake on Drew Field in the 1940s. These men could then use this newfound experience to go fishing on the weekend. Landing huge jewfish off the Mullet Key Gunnery Range became a competitive sport for MacDill's men during the war—while it was not actively being bombed of course. (Courtesy 6 AMW/HO.)

The Army Air Corps Trains in Florida

A pilot mounts his bird in this 1940s postcard. Pilots learned to fly at army flight schools and were proficient with their plane prior to arriving at MacDill. It was on MacDill that the bomber crews were molded into a fighting team. Having after-hours beers together certainly helped promote camaraderie as well (only beer though, as the War Department prohibited the sale of liquor at Army posts in 1944). (Courtesy author.)

A group of MacDill officers and enlisted personnel pose for a portrait on February 4, 1945. An integral element of the bomber crew was the aerial (or flight) engineers, who served as airborne mechanics should any problems arise in flight. Seated behind the pilots, they monitored the auxiliary and oxygen systems, the fuel transfer and electrical systems, voltage readings, and fuse locations and performed emergency airborne repairs. (Courtesy HCPL.)

110—Air Corps in Review at Mac Dill Field, Tampa, Fla.

PHOTO BY U.S. ARMY AIR CORPS
19-H1101

A 1940s postcard depicts officers and enlisted men marching in review with B-17s buzzing about overhead. MacDill's 11th Photo Group used bombers like these for their globe-trotting mapping missions. Using three wide-angle lenses mounted around the aircraft's nose, the planes would take near-continuous pictures from horizon to horizon, snapping thousands of rolls of film during a single mission. (Courtesy author.)

MacDill Field officers and men stand in front of a Boeing B-29 Superfortress about 1947. Entering service in June 1943 and deploying on combat missions in June 1944, virtually all of the massive bombers' first missions were launched from newly constructed air bases in the Pacific built by some of the same engineers who received their initial training on MacDill. (Courtesy 6 AMW/HO.)

A Boeing B-29 Superfortress takes off from MacDill Field about 1947. The Superfortresses arrived on MacDill postwar in late 1945, during a transitional period in MacDill's history (as well as America's on a whole). A contingent of P-51 Mustangs, looking miniscule next to these goliaths, also arrived on MacDill during this period. (Courtesy 6 AMW/HO.)

B-29 Superfortresses are seen flying in formation over MacDill Field about 1947. The massive bombers featured four 2,200-horsepower engines and had a staggering wingspan of 141 feet (compared to the B-17's wingspan of 103 feet). The B-29 was the first bomber to feature a pressurized cabin. (Courtesy 6 AMW/HO.)

Boeing B-29 Superfortresses sit along the flight line on MacDill Field about 1947. During this year, on July 26, 1947, the US Air Force was born, and MacDill Field was renamed MacDill Air Force Base. (Official Army Air Corps photograph; courtesy *Tampa Tribune*.)

A mosaic of MacDill Field is captured some time in the late 1940s (postwar). B-29s can be seen parked along the hangar line. Other than the main area of the base and the hospital complex at the southern tip of the peninsula (the location of MacDill's modern-day marina), vast expanses of the base remain desolate. (Courtesy 6 AMW/HO.)

A mixture of Martin B-26 Marauders, Boeing B-17 Flying Fortresses, B-29 Superfortresses, and Douglas C-47 "Gooney Birds" can be seen crowding MacDill's aprons in this photograph captured on August 7, 1949. Following the cessation of World War II hostilities, MacDill began training bomber pilots and crews on the transition from Flying Fortresses and Marauders to the B-29s.

MacDill's rail line can be seen weaving its way through the base, with fuel cars visible in the lower right. MacDill shouldered a tremendous burden during the war, and the pilots and crewmen who trained on the base flew combat missions in every operational theater of war. (Official Army Air Corps photograph; courtesy *Tampa Tribune*.)

The pandemonium that was present on MacDill's hangar line during the war—ordnance specialists loading bombs and ammunition, fuel trucks racing to and from, and mechanics zipping around with grease guns—had all but subsided by the late 1940s. MacDill's cryptographers were no longer studying German and Japanese codes, the threat from U-boats had receded, and WAC photo technicians were no longer interpreting mosaics of Fortress Europe. Marriages continued at MacDill's two chapels, Army chaplains visited the sick and advised the distressed, and troops enjoyed fishing from the hospital docks and picnicking along Indian Rocks Beach. Recovering troops convalesced at the Don Cesar on St. Petersburg Beach. Enlisted men and civilian clerks continued to requisition supplies, and MacDill's Rationing Office carried on with mending worn clothes and repairing shoes. Meanwhile, across the Atlantic, American cargo planes were delivering supplies to starving Germans cut off by the Soviets. Many of the same American pilots who had bombed Berlin were now releasing candy from their weapon bays to grateful German children. The once-Allied Soviets were allies no more. (Courtesy TBHC.)

Three

DETERRING THE RED MENACE

In 1950, Tampa was referred to as "Florida's Gulf Coast Metropolis." It had a census population of 124,073 within city limits and 201,629 within a 10-mile radius of downtown. Tampa was Florida's principal industrial city and led the nation with its production of the world-famous, handmade Havana cigars. An estimated 67 percent of Florida's citrus was produced in the immediate area, which was the citrus canning capital of the world. Every year, members of Ye Mystic Krewe of Gasparilla descended on the city, sailing their pirate ships in a mock invasion of Tampa, followed by a street parade and a trip to the Florida State Fair.

At the end of World War II, with as many as 15 million troops returning from overseas assignments, America experienced a significant housing shortage. As the Soviet threat increased, the armed services sought to retain vast numbers of experienced veterans, especially those experienced in highly technical fields, including missile systems and nuclear armaments. On March 5, 1949, Sen. Kenneth Wherry, of Nebraska, sponsored a bill to provide adequate family housing on or near military installations, the result of which became known as Wherry Housing, and MacDill would see its share.

As of September 1951, MacDill had become an asset of the Strategic Air Command (SAC), and MacDill's major tenant units included the 6th Air Division; the 305th, 306th, and 307th Bombardment Wings; and the 306th Combat Support Group. In October 1951, MacDill's 306th Bombardment Wing became the first operational Boeing B-47 Stratojet wing in America, and the base would eventually host over 50 of these jet bombers. MacDill's 305th and 306th Bomb Wings were continuously setting and then breaking world records in their B-47s for flight times across the Atlantic. Col. Michael N.W. McCoy, commander of MacDill's 306th Bomb Wing, established the first record in April 1953, when he flew the nearly 3,000-mile route from Limestone, Maine, to Fairford, England, in 5 hours and 53 minutes.

A Wherry housing project is being built on the east side of MacDill on June 25, 1950. The billets, named the Tampa Bay Gardens Apartments, included officer and enlisted family housing as well as Bachelor Officer Quarters (BOQ), Visiting Officer Quarters (VOQ), and a guesthouse for temporary lodging. Starting rent was $52.50 a month, with no deposit required. (Courtesy 6 AMW/HO.)

The Tampa Bay Gardens Apartments offered "comfortable, convenient, economical housing in attractive surroundings" and featured 16 children's playgrounds, laundry facilities, bus transportation, and door-to-door mail delivery. The residences featured the "advantages" of all-electric kitchens, space heaters, and venetian blinds and were available in homes, duplexes, and multi-room apartments, furnished and unfurnished. (Courtesy 6 AMW/HO.)

Maj. Gen. Frank A. Armstrong Jr. (left), who assumed command of the 6th Air Division on MacDill in May 1951, and Col. Brintnall H. Merchant, who became MacDill's base commander in August 1951, are pictured reviewing the annual base programming plan in September 1951. With the Korean War undoubtedly on the forefront of their discussion, MacDill's base preparedness was a prime concern. (Courtesy 6 AMW/HO.)

Col. Donald Hillman (left), deputy commander of the 306th Bombardment Wing, inspects the construction of a KC-97 Stratotanker nose dock with an unidentified officer on MacDill on August 24, 1951. Hillman served under Col. Michael N.W. McCoy, commander of the 306th Bomb Wing. It was under McCoy that MacDill received its first jet bombers, the B-47s, in October 1951. (Courtesy 6 AMW/HO.)

Col. Donald Hillman is pictured in the canopy of one of MacDill's new Boeing B-47 Stratojets about 1952. MacDill's 306th Bomb Wing was the first in America to be assigned the radical new bombers, and the 306th was cited at the time as being the most modern all-jet wing in the world. Part of the 306th's mission became training pilots on the new bombers. (Courtesy 6 AMW/HO.)

B-47 bombers and KC-97 tankers mingle on MacDill's tarmac about 1952. Both the 305th and 306th Bombardment Wings were assigned squadrons of the KC-97s (the 305th and 306th Aerial Refueling Squadrons, respectively), as Strategic Air Command's responsibilities encompassed not only strategic bombardment but also aerial refueling missions. The KC-97s would remain at MacDill until 1962. (Courtesy 6 AMW/HO.)

The Boeing KC-97 Stratotanker, pictured on MacDill in 1951, was originally designed as a cargo and personnel transport equivalent to Boeing's B-29 Superfortress, with a second fuselage being added to the aircraft's body. Under the Strategic Air Command, it was converted to its role as an aerial tanker to transfer fuel to SAC's bombers and fighters flying long-range strike packages. (Courtesy 6 AMW/HO.)

Boeing B-47 Stratojet bombers fly in formation over a MacDill hangar about 1951. The B-47 was America's first swept-wing jet bomber, could reach speeds of just over 600 miles per hour, could carry a 25,000-pound bomb load, and was armed with two rear-facing, 20-millimeter cannons. Equipped with refueling receptacles, B-47s became the bomber of choice for the long-range bombing missions required by SAC. (Courtesy 6 AMW/HO.)

Employees—one looking rather grim—await eager customers at the MacDill (misspelled on sign) Officers' Open Mess on October 10, 1951. The Officers' Mess membership dues were $5 per month for bachelors and 50¢ more per month for married officers. For the enlisted, there was the NCO Open Mess, which featured a bar, package sales, lounge, and short order mess. Membership fees for full participation were $1 per month. (Courtesy USF.)

The Military Exchange, pictured on August 21, 1951, was located off base on MacDill Avenue. The business catered to troops, offering discounted prices on alterations and insignias. On base, airmen could use the base laundry facilities to have their uniforms laundered for a flat rate of 50¢ for 12 pieces, or $1 for 25 pieces. (Courtesy HCPL.)

Revelers enjoy the 1952 New Year's Day reception at MacDill's Officers' Club, hosted by Maj. Gen. Frank A. Armstrong, commander of the 6th Air Division, and his wife (second and third from left). Also present were, from left to right, Col. and Mrs. Elliot Vandevanter, Col. and Mrs. Brintnall H. Merchant, and Col. and Mrs. Michael N.W. McCoy. (Courtesy 6 AMW/HO.)

Major General Armstrong (second from left, and sporting a rather meek-looking sidearm), along with several unidentified colonels, greet Maj. Gen. Joseph H. Atkinson (left), commander of the Second Air Force, headquartered at Barksdale AFB, Louisiana, for an informal inspection visit about 1952. A KC-97 is visible to the left. (Courtesy 6 AMW/HO.)

Maj. Gen. Frank A. Armstrong (left) and Col. Brintnall H. Merchant (center), MacDill's base commander, greet (and admire the crisp uniform of) an unidentified four-star on MacDill's tarmac in front of a B-47 about 1952. Because of the importance of the B-47 mission within Strategic Air Command, MacDill routinely found itself being visited by high-ranking brass. (Courtesy 6 AMW/HO.)

Major General Armstrong (center) and Colonel Merchant (far right) welcome unidentified Tampa civilians onto MacDill for tours and a base review about 1952. In 1942, Armstrong led the first ever US Army Air Corps daylight raid over occupied Europe, pounding targets within France while suffering no losses during the mission. Armstrong was awarded the Silver Star for the operation. (Courtesy 6 AMW/HO.)

On November 16, 1952, Major General Armstrong was reassigned to command the Second Air Force at Barksdale AFB. Pictured is the change of command ceremony, where Brig. Gen. Henry K. Mooney (front right) assumed command of the 6th from Armstrong (front left). Also pictured are Colonel Vandevanter, 305th Bomb Wing commander; Colonel Merchant, base commander; Colonel McCoy, 306th Bomb Wing commander; and Col. John H. Kunkel Jr., commander, OTU. (Courtesy 6 AMW/HO.)

After receiving a briefing on MacDill's activities, Assistant Secretary of the Air Force Harold Stewart (second from left) is shown conferring with Col. John A. Hilger of the 306th Bomb Wing (left), Col. John P. Proctor of the 305th Bomb Wing (second from right), and Col. Brintnall H. Merchant, base commander (right) about 1953. (Courtesy 6 AMW/HO.)

A 1953 postcard depicts B-47s parked along MacDill's apron. Between 1947 and 1956, over 2,000 B-47s (including multiple variants) were built and distributed to USAF bomb wings throughout America under the Strategic Air Command. No doubt many hours were spent behind the Soviet Union's Iron Curtain studying reconnaissance photographs of the B-47s on MacDill. (Courtesy author.)

Members of MacDill's 8th Crash Reserve Boat Flight perform maintenance on the radar of a USAF P-38 crash rescue boat in 1953. No longer soldier-sailors, the USAF airmen-sailors took over where the Army's World War II–era Quartermaster Boat Company left off—always at the ready to rescue downed pilots and crew in Hillsborough Bay or the Gulf of Mexico. (Courtesy 6 AMW/HO.)

The USAF crash rescue boats, like their Army brethren before them, were also used to court and ferry distinguished guests who visited MacDill, as pictured here in 1953. The MacDill Navy diminished during the 1950s, as a squadron of Kaman HH-43 Huskie helicopters arrived in 1953 to assume MacDill's search-and-rescue mission. Fishing for jewfish from these new rescue platforms would have been difficult. (Courtesy 6 AMW/HO.)

A USAF crash rescue boat (the same boat as in the previous image) suffers irreparable harm after being engulfed by flames about 1953. MacDill firefighters are seen battling the blaze from the dock as the boat's Old Glory waves on defiantly. Following the devastating fire, the ship was sent to Davy Jones's locker. (Courtesy 6 AMW/HO.)

Enlisted men and officers (including one in Bermuda shorts) sort and inspect the contents of MacDill's base supply in the 1950s. When not working, airmen and officers in the 1950s could engage in various free-time activities around the base, including at the Photo or Woodworking Hobby Shop, at the Automotive Shop, or by joining the Pistol or Motorcycle Clubs. (Courtesy 6 AMW/HO.)

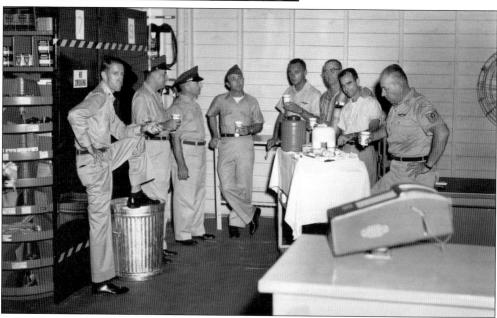

Enlisted men and officers of the Base Supply Squadron take a coffee break and enjoy some conversation in the 1950s. The Wingspread Cafeteria and Beer Bar remained open for business from the frantic days of World War II. The 1950s base newspaper, the *Airman*, was prepared by the staff of MacDill's Information Services Office and distributed throughout the base every Friday without charge to base personnel. (Courtesy 6 AMW/HO.)

Lt. Col. George Snyder, of base supply, performs an inspection at one of MacDill's distribution points in the 1950s. Tomato sauce and Danish sardines were apparently on the menu. After dinner, sports-minded MacDill personnel could enjoy the field's baseball diamond, five softball diamonds, six cement tennis courts, two swimming pools, or the fish camp near the hospital. (Courtesy 6 AMW/HO.)

Pictured in the 1950s, Lt. Col. George Snyder checks in more sardines. MacDill would also become well known for its excellent golf course, which in the 1950s was open to all base personnel for monthly dues of only $3. The greens fee for nonmembers was 75¢ for unlimited play, and golf clubs could be rented for 50¢ per day. (Courtesy 6 AMW/HO.)

After a three-month training mission in Fairford, England, Col. Michael N.W. McCoy, commander of the 306th Bomb Wing, reviews a written notification with wing adjutant Maj. J.W. Whitaker. The notice announces the planned return of the wing and its squadron of B-47s to its home station at MacDill AFB in September 1953. (Courtesy 6 AMW/HO.)

Men and officers of the 306th Bomb Wing, some carrying carbines, are shown boarding a USAF transport on September 5, 1953, for their return trip to MacDill AFB after completing their training mission in Fairford, England. The B-47, regarded at the time as the world's fastest bomber, no doubt made quite an impression on the RAF. (Courtesy 6 AMW/HO.)

A 306th Bomb Wing B-47 blasts off the runway of Fairford Field, England, on its return flight to MacDill AFB on September 5, 1953. With its flight of B-47s from MacDill AFB to England on June 4, 1953, the 306th set a world record for the fastest nonstop flight across the Atlantic. Colonel McCoy piloted the lead plane into the history books. (Courtesy 6 AMW/HO.)

McCoy (right) discusses a flight with a fellow crewman on MacDill's tarmac in about 1953. After leaving MacDill, McCoy assumed command of a B-47 wing at Pinecastle AFB, Florida. Tragically, McCoy was killed while piloting a B-47 that crashed 15 miles northeast of Orlando on October 9, 1957. Pinecastle AFB was renamed McCoy AFB a few months after the crash; it became Orlando International Airport in the 1970s. (Courtesy 6 AMW/HO.)

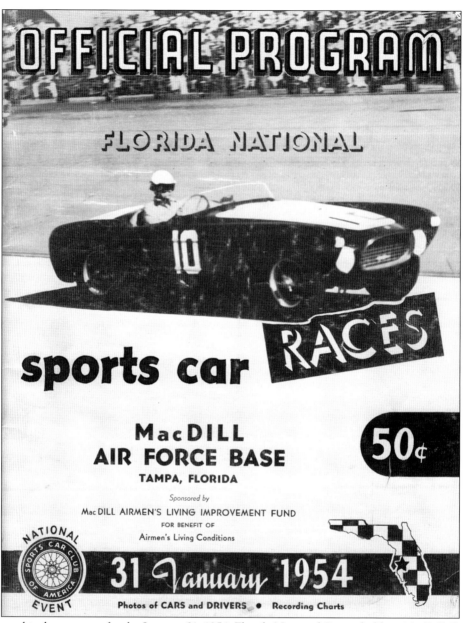

OFFICIAL PROGRAM

FLORIDA NATIONAL

sports car RACES

MacDILL AIR FORCE BASE
TAMPA, FLORIDA

Sponsored by
MacDILL AIRMEN'S LIVING IMPROVEMENT FUND
FOR BENEFIT OF
Airmen's Living Conditions

50¢

NATIONAL SPORTS CAR CLUB OF AMERICA EVENT

31 January 1954

Photos of CARS and DRIVERS • Recording Charts

Pictured is the program for the January 31, 1954, Florida National Races, held on MacDill. Race officials included Brig. Gen. Henry K. Mooney, commander of the 6th Air Division; Brig. Gen. Hewitt T. Wheless, commander of the 306th Bomb Wing; Col. Elliott Vandevanter Jr., commander of the 305th Bomb Wing; and Col. Brintnall H. Merchant, MacDill base commander. The NCO Open Mess was open to the spectators, and fans could get a hamburger and fries for 25¢ or a T-bone steak for $1.25. Drinks included the Ferrari Fizzler and the Daimler Daiquiri for 40¢, or the M.G. Manhattan or the Maserati Martini for 45¢. The base wings each nominated their own bathing beauties to participate in the Sports Car Queen of '54 beauty contest. Tampa Florida Brewery, Inc.'s Tropical Extra Fine Ale (with the motto, "For the Lift that Lasts, Ask for Tropical") was available to the fans, as was Tampa's Southern Brewing Company's Silver Bar Premium Lager, which boasted, "if you had a million dollars you couldn't buy a better beer." (Courtesy author.)

The 1954 race included the Imperial Polk County Race for cars under 1,500 cubic centimeters; the Festival of States Race for cars over 1,500 cubic centimeters; the Gasparilla Trophy Race for production cars; and the Governor Dan McCarty Memorial Race, a grueling 200-mile, winner-take-all race of attrition available to all classes. The race was attended by none other than Gen. Curtis "Bombs Away" LeMay, SAC commander. (Photograph by E.L. Eveleth; courtesy author.)

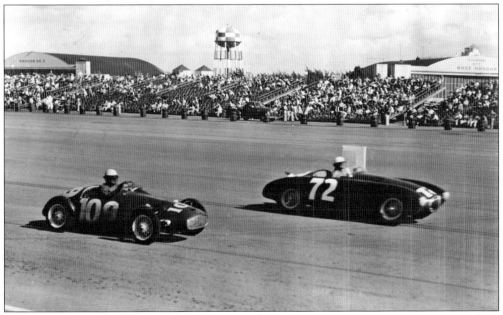

Sponsored by the Sports Car Club of America and using the runways as tracks, the proceeds from the 1953 and 1954 races went towards the MacDill Airmen's Living Improvement Fund to benefit on-base living conditions and amenities. During a six-hour grudge match over a 4.2-mile course on February 21, 1953, John Fitch, *Speed Age* Sport Car Driver of the Year, gunned a Cunningham to victory, covering 492 miles before capturing the checkered flag. (Courtesy 6 AMW/HO.)

One of the benefits of the proceeds earned from the races was the fabulous Beach Park on the eastern side of the MacDill peninsula, shown about 1954. One of the sponsors, United Aircraft Corporation, correctly noted, "Every citizen—and indeed the entire free world—can be grateful for the Strategic Air Command, America's great air-striking force which has been such a powerful deterrent to world aggression." (Courtesy 6 AMW/HO.)

An aerial view of MacDill's squadron hospital complex and grounds, along with the base marina, is captured on September 15, 1954. When not fishing, MacDill personnel enjoyed attending other area attractions, including Major League Baseball spring training games, Cypress Gardens, the Ringling Museum in Sarasota, the Bok Singing Tower and Bird Sanctuary in Lake Wales, and the Sponge Docks in Tarpon Springs. (Courtesy HCPL.)

"Luxurious" base housing is pictured in the 1950s. Expanded base amenities included a skeet range (membership required), two movie theaters, and the new MacDill Education Office, where personnel could take courses through an extension of Lakeland's Florida Southern College, the USAF Extension Course Institute, or the USAF Institute of Technology. The Tinker Elementary School also opened for dependents, and two swimming pools offered a way to beat the Florida heat. (Courtesy 6 AMW/HO.)

Taken on September 14, 1954, this picture shows an aerial view of MacDill's Tampa Bay Gardens Apartments complex. During the late 1950s, improved base services included a renovated and expanded base Fish Camp, which offered over 20 skiffs (measuring 15–17 feet) as well as several passenger boats for families. Fishing for speckled and silver trout, redfish, grouper, and mackerel in Hillsborough Bay became a popular pastime for the expanding number of on-base residents. (Courtesy HCPL.)

The traveler's check window at the First National Bank of Tampa, MacDill AFB Branch, is shown on November 25, 1957. The First National Bank had a branch office located in the center of MacDill's administrative complex. The branch provided usual banking to MacDill personnel, including checking and savings accounts and the issuance of traveler's checks. (Courtesy HCPL.)

The First National Bank, MacDill AFB Branch, included a personal-check-cashing window where a friendly teller could always be found waiting to disperse some funds. The branch was open Monday through Saturday and offered extended hours on Friday and paydays. Airmen could obtain safe deposit boxes through MacDill's Personal Affairs Section. (Courtesy HCPL.)

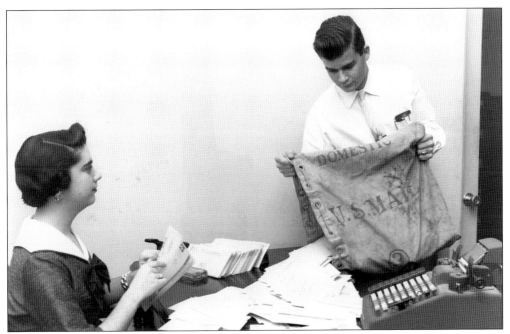

A dapper young man delivers night deposits to a seemingly inundated desk clerk at the First National Bank of Tampa, MacDill AFB Branch, on November 25, 1957. Both the Officers' Open Mess and the NCO Open Mess included check-cashing privileges as a portion of their membership dues, though the checks could not exceed $50, which was considered a substantial amount at the time. (Courtesy HCPL.)

Tellers and customers interact at the First National Bank on November 25, 1957. On paydays, airmen were eager to cash their checks and head across the six-mile stretch of Gandy Bridge, one of the longest spans in the country at the time, to hit the beaches of Clearwater and St. Petersburg. (Courtesy HCPL.)

The construction of a new base hospital, pictured here, began in 1956, and it was completed the following year. Located near the Tampa Bay Gardens Apartments, the hospital's new location was much more convenient for the airmen and their dependants. Shortly thereafter, new airmen dorms were under construction (completed in 1960), and an expansion was made to the Base Exchange (BX). (Courtesy 6 AMW/HO.)

MacDill's hospital was open and accepting patients in 1957. The American Red Cross maintained a branch office and a recreational lounge at the base hospital to assist with the patients. A vast expansion project was also underway at the golf course, where enthusiasts enjoyed a brand new, 250-yard driving range. (Courtesy 6 AMW/HO.)

Four

NAPALM AND

NATION BUILDING

Gen. Paul W. Tibbets Jr., previously mentioned in this book as the MacDill-trained bomber and the pilot of the *Enola Gay*, returned to MacDill in January 1958 and assumed command of the 6th Air Division, a position he held until February 1961. US Strike Command (USSTRICOM) was established on MacDill Air Force Base on October 9, 1961, and had a global mission of supplying war-fighters anywhere in the world. STRICOM was the first unified combatant command to be hosted by MacDill, but it certainly would not be the last; it was followed later by US Readiness Command, US Central Command, and US Special Operations Command. Benjamin O. Davis Jr., identified earlier, served as a deputy commander of STRICOM from August 1968 to February 1970.

The 15th Tactical Fighter Wing (TFW) was activated on MacDill on July 1, 1962, and was designated as MacDill's parent wing, a position it held until 1970, when it was replaced by the 1st Tactical Fighter Wing. Its first commander was Col. George L. Jones, who oversaw the conversion on MacDill from the Republic F-84F Thunderstreak fighters to the McDonnell F-4 Phantom IIs. By 1963, MacDill had been transferred from Strategic Air Command to Tactical Air Command. In November 1965, MacDill's 15th and 12th Tactical Fighter Wings deployed to Southeast Asia, flying F-4 Phantom II combat operations from Cam Ranh Bay, South Vietnam, and Ubon Royal Thai Air Base, in Thailand. The F-4 pilots, often escorting Republic F-105 Thunderchiefs ("Thuds") on hunter-killer missions, flew route packs over North Vietnam, including the deadly Route Pack Six, which brought pilots on bombing runs over Hanoi. The F-4 Phantom II served as an air superiority and interdiction fighter, though it excelled in a multitude of roles, including providing close air support to American ground forces engaged with the enemy, destroying ground-based targets of opportunity, and performing intelligence, surveillance, and reconnaissance missions over both friendly and enemy territory.

In 1991, MacDill was again a target of military downsizing, and by April 1, 1994, MacDill's 56th Tactical Fighter Wing (later Tactical Training Wing), which was established as MacDill's host unit on June 1, 1975, and oversaw a substantial percentage of all USAF pilot training on the new F-16 Fighting Falcons, had transferred to Luke Air Force Base, Arizona.

Department of Defense (DoD) plans to close MacDill, shown here on November 29, 1960, began to percolate during 1960 because of high operating costs and the need for substantial rehabilitation. Initial plans proposed by the DoD called for MacDill to be closed by June 1962. World events, however, reversed this decision. During the Cuban Missile Crisis, MacDill accommodated over 300 strike aircraft. (Courtesy author.)

Pictured is the original artist's rendering from about 1961 of what would later become the official insignia for US Strike Command (USSTRICOM), activated on MacDill on October 9, 1961. At the urging of Pres. John F. Kennedy, the Joint Chiefs of Staff conducted an extensive study of American capabilities and recommended the need to establish a new unified command of combat-ready forces that could be "swift, effective, and flexible." (Courtesy 6 AMW/HO.)

This aerial view of MacDill was taken on October 24, 1962, just 10 days after an American U-2 photograph reconnaissance mission collected irrefutable evidence that the Soviets were covertly assembling platforms on Cuba to host medium- and intermediate-range ballistic nuclear missiles. As war planners envisioned everything from a conventional invasion of Cuba to a global nuclear conflagration, MacDill became a staging ground for strike aircraft assets. (Courtesy author.)

Standing in front of a B-47 Stratojet, armed guards of MacDill's Combat Defense Force pose as they secure the flight line in the 1960s. As MacDill remained an asset of Strategic Air Command, strategic bombers and aerial refueling tankers were left on 24-hour alert because of the threat of a Soviet nuclear strike. (Courtesy 6 AMW/HO.)

Crewmen respond to a SAC alert as they rush to their B-47 about 1963. In January 1960, a new alert facility was constructed along the southern end of one of MacDill's runways. Including crew quarters, a briefing room, lounges, and a dining hall, the facility was meant to reduce the reaction time needed to respond to a global emergency. (Courtesy 6 AMW/HO.)

This March 15, 1963, photograph includes, from left to right, Col. Brintnall H. Merchant, retired base commander; Scott Christopher, executive vice president of the Tampa Chamber of Commerce; Col. Stanley I. Hand, commander of the 306th Bombardment Wing; Mayor Julian Lane of Tampa; and Arthur Brown, Military Affairs Committeeman of the Tampa Chamber of Commerce. The group poses with the 306th Bomb Wing's "City of Tampa" B-47. (Courtesy 6 AMW/HO.)

March 15, 1963, marked the day MacDill's last B-47 Stratojet departed for its final resting place in storage at Davis-Monthan AFB. The event was open to the public and was attended by local residents and dignitaries. God-fearing parishioners from the First Baptist Church of Tampa are shown posing with an "angel of death" that is most likely not recognized by their theologians or orthodoxy. (Courtesy 6 AMW/HO.)

Tourists from Sweden and Norway, escorted by MacDill representatives, stand admiring American firepower in the shadow of a B-47 Stratojet on March 15, 1963. The Norwegians are reminded of the benefits of being allied with the United States, within the NATO alliance, and being protected by America's nuclear umbrella. (Courtesy 6 AMW/HO.)

Lt. Col. Albert H. Holman signifies that he was the first of his class at MacDill Air Force Base to solo in a Republic F-84F Thunderstreak fighter, which arrived on MacDill in 1962. The first class consisted of 20 men participating in an eight-week course, which included instruction in formation flying, aerial refueling, instrument training, and gunnery practice. (Official USAF photograph; courtesy *Tampa Tribune*.)

An unidentified F-84F Thunderstreak pilot and crewman debrief following a training flight on September 20, 1963. The Thunderstreak was the offspring of the Republic F-84E Thunderjet, America's primary fighter during the Korean War, though the newer Thunderstreak featured a new swept-back wing design. The Thunderstreak entered service as an asset of SAC with the purpose of escorting long-range bombers. (Official USAF photograph; courtesy *Tampa Tribune*.)

Capt. Dumitru Tokanel (right) is congratulated by Maj. J.F. Smith after completing his first solo mission in an F-84F on September 11, 1963, while a proud instructor, Capt. Don Friesen, looks on. Armed with six Browning machine guns, the Thunderstreak was a welcome escort to SAC bombers circling over the frigid waters of the North Atlantic. (Official USAF photograph; courtesy *Tampa Tribune*.)

A group of F-84F Thunderstreak fighter escorts sits carefully arranged on MacDill's tarmac in August 1964. By this time, MacDill AFB had been transferred from SAC to Tactical Air Command (TAC). Interestingly, when TAC was first activated on March 21, 1946, a headquarters for the new command was briefly located on MacDill. (Official USAF photograph; courtesy *Tampa Tribune*.)

Capt. Jack D. Gravis (left) is congratulated by Col. Oakley W. Baron, 15th Tactical Fighter Wing deputy for operations, as he descends from his F-84F in 1964. Captain Gravis was the last student to complete the F-84F training program under the 45th Tactical Fighter Squadron (TFS). Looking on is Lt. Col. Ivan L. McGuire, commander of the 45th TFS at the time. (Courtesy 6 AMW/HO.)

Civilians review an F-84F and its static armament and ordnance displays during an open house on MacDill about 1964, and a long line forms of those eager to take a peek into the cockpit. The Thunderstreak was able to carry a bomb load of 6,000 pounds on four underwing pylons and was capable of reaching speeds in excess of 650 miles per hour. (Courtesy 6 AMW/HO.)

Although the 12th Tactical Fighting Wing had been operating the McDonnell Douglas F-4B Phantom II model since February 1963, it was not until June 1964 that the 15th Tactical Fighter Wing (TFW) received the newer F-4C models. Here, Col. Francis J. Vetort (left), commander of the 15th TFW, and Capt. Carmine A. Vito prepare to fly the wing's first new Phantom model. (Courtesy 6 AMW/HO.)

A crew chief helps guide a pilot and his F-4C on MacDill's apron in December 1964. At the time, the F-4C was America's fastest and highest-flying all-weather fighter bomber, with two engines and a two-man crew. The top speed exceeded 1,400 miles per hour, and it had flown to an altitude of nearly 100,000 feet during initial tests. (Official USAF photograph; courtesy *Tampa Tribune*.)

F-4C pilots huddle on MacDill's tarmac to watch one of their own paint a star on his Phantom in the 1960s. With reserve tanks, the F-4C could push past 2,000 miles. The two J79-15 engines were started using a cartridge or pneumatic starter and produced 34,000 pounds of thrust in afterburner. The F-4C's air-to-air intercept capabilities extended beyond 900 miles, and its air-to-ground attack capability was devastating. (Courtesy 6 AMW/HO.)

Visiting from Ethiopia, 16 newsmen react to F-4Cs zooming overhead while admiring a static display of their firepower during a 1966 MacDill air show. Members of the British Parliament were also distinguished visitors, as the foreigners received tours of the base and were permitted to photograph the static displays. (Courtesy 6 AMW/HO.)

A 1960s aerial view of MacDill AFB shows F-4C Phantom IIs crowding the aprons. The F-4Cs could carry an incredible amount and array of air-to-air and air-to-ground ordnance in multiple rocket packages, wing stations, and armament racks, up to as much as 16,000 pounds. The Phantom IIs, unlike the Thunderstreaks, had a crew of two: a pilot and a weapon-systems officer (WSO). (Courtesy 6 AMW/HO.)

In May 1966, MacDill dedicated a new road in honor of Col. Harold M. McClelland, who died while in command of MacDill's 12th Tactical Fighter Wing in May 1962. His widow and his son Michael C. McClelland accompany Brig. Gen. Frank Collins, commander of the 836th Air Division, during the ceremony. (Courtesy 6 AMW/HO.)

An F-4C Phantom II pilot sits deep in thought about 1967. Phantoms operated the largest fighter radar antenna available at the time and were capable of detecting enemy fighters at enormous ranges. Their thrust ratio allowed takeoffs using less than 5,000 feet of runway. Although the fastest fighter at the time, it also held the record for flying the slowest, providing it exceptional short landing capabilities. (Courtesy 6 AMW/HO.)

MacDill was open to the public on October 21, 1967, for the Kiwanis Kids' Day Open House. Civilians were permitted to enjoy static displays of fighters, bombers, and ordnance. Note the massive B-52 lurking in the background. Although MacDill had been transferred from Strategic Air Command (SAC) to Tactical Air Command (TAC), SAC did maintain assets on MacDill throughout the 1960s (though not B-52s). (Courtesy 6 AMW/HO.)

It's Kiwanis Kids' Day Open House at MacDill! Children frolic around a MacDill-based Bell UH-1 Huey on October 21, 1967. Just three months after this picture was taken, choppers like this would be engaging and destroying North Vietnamese and Viet Cong regulars and guerrillas during the Communists' failed Tet Offensive. (Courtesy 6 AMW/HO.)

A Huey is seen maneuvering along MacDill in the 1960s. Although ubiquitous throughout America's armed forces during the 1960s as a multirole helicopter, the Hueys would later become an important part of MacDill in 1975, when the 56th Tactical Fighter Wing arrived and assumed responsibilities over the 100,000-plus-acre Avon Park Air Force Range. (Courtesy 6 AMW/HO.)

An aerial view shows F-4Cs parked along MacDill's aprons in the 1960s. In December 1964, four MacDill-based F-4Cs from the 12th Tactical Fighter Wing set an unofficial world fighter endurance record by flying an 18-hour deployment flight. Within the same month, MacDill deployed its first squadron of the F-4Cs to Okinawa, Japan. (Courtesy 6 AMW/HO.)

On July 10, 1965, the previously MacDill-based 45th Tactical Fighter Squadron, under the 15th Tactical Fighter Wing, produced the first USAF air-to-air kills since the Korean War by vaporizing two North Vietnamese Soviet-made MIG-17s over Vietnam. Armed with radar-guided Sparrow III air-to-air missiles, infrared-guided Sidewinder missiles, bombs, mines, and 150-gallon napalm canisters, the Phantom IIs were a force to be reckoned with. (Courtesy 6 AMW/HO.)

The 1st Tactical Fighter Wing arrived on MacDill on January 10, 1970, and replaced the 15th TFW as MacDill's host unit. On July 1, 1971, it held a Re-dedication Day, in which the previously named 45th, 46th, and 47th Tactical Fighter Squadrons became the 27th, 94th, and 71st Tactical Fighter Squadrons, in line with the designations of the historic 1st Pursuit Group from World War I. (Courtesy 6 AMW/HO.)

The July 1, 1971, Re-dedication Day was attended by none other than fighter ace and Medal of Honor recipient Capt. Eddie Rickenbacker (right). A race car driver prior to entering the service, Rickenbacker started his US Army career as a chauffeur to Gen. John J. Pershing. By the end of World War I, Rickenbacker had become America's leading ace with 26 confirmed kills: 22 enemy aircraft and 4 enemy balloons. (Courtesy 6 AMW/HO.)

Pictured is the original artist's rendering of the insignia for US Readiness Command (USREDCOM), which activated on MacDill in January 1972 and was essentially just a redesignation of USSTRICOM, which then ceased to exist. REDCOM, upon activation, took over STRICOM's facility on MacDill, which had been built for the command in 1968. (Courtesy 6 AMW/HO.)

The US Readiness Command Headquarters appears about 1972. STRICOM's first commander, Gen. Paul D. Adams, also concurrently served as the commander of the Middle East, Africa (south of the Sahara), and southern Asia (MEAFSA), and with this additional duty, was responsible for all American defense interests and activities within these geographical areas. When STRICOM was redesignated REDCOM, the responsibility for these areas was terminated. (Courtesy USF.)

An aerial view of MacDill, taken in 1972, shows over 30 years of expansion. The building that would consecutively serve as the headquarters for STRICOM, REDCOM, and the US Special Operations Command can be seen; however, the area that would later become the headquarters for US Central Command is still nothing more than a grass field. (Courtesy 6 AMW/HO.)

Col. Henry D. Cantebury, who assumed command of the 56th Tactical Fighter Wing on MacDill in July 1979, addresses a crowd of base personnel in October 1979 in front of one of MacDill's brand new F-16s. Under Cantebury, MacDill's Tactical Air Command mission became training fighter pilots on the USAF's new air supremacy fighter. The 56th TFW replaced the 1st TFW on June 1, 1975. (Courtesy 6 AMW/HO.)

Sr. Amn. Raymond J. Buszek (left), an aircraft armament system specialist, is shown thanking Maj. James B. Barton, chief of the Quality Assurance Division, for an orientation ride aboard an F-4D model Phantom II. The two flew the last F-4D mission under MacDill's 61st Tactical Fighting Squadron on November 19, 1979. The squadron was a unit of the 56th Tactical Fighter Wing. (Courtesy 6 AMW/HO.)

A General Dynamics F-16A Fighting Falcon, of the 56th Tactical Training Wing (TTW), is shown flying along Florida's coast on June 1, 1983. The year 1982 marked the last year that the F-4 Phantom IIs were stationed on MacDill, with the 56th Tactical Fighter Wing being redesignated as the 56th Tactical Training Wing (TTW) and becoming a fully operational F-16 wing. (Official USAF photograph, courtesy defenseimagery.mil.)

A 56th TTW F-16 travels between MacDill and the Avon Park Air Force Range on August 16, 1983. Between 1979 and 1993, as many as half of all USAF F-16 pilots and numerous F-16 pilots of allied nations were trained on MacDill under the 56th TTW—many of them flew combat missions over Iraq and Kuwait during Operations Desert Shield and Desert Storm. (Official USAF photograph; courtesy defenseimagery.mil.)

The responsibilities for military planning and contingencies in the Middle East, Africa, and southern Asia (MEAFSA), which were purged when STRICOM became REDCOM, were later assumed by the Rapid Deployment Joint Task Force (RDJTF) when it was activated on MacDill in March 1980. RDJTF remained a subordinate of REDCOM until January 1, 1983, when it became a separate unified combatant command, known as US Central Command (USCENTCOM). (Courtesy 6 AMW/HO.)

The responsibilities for prosecuting 1991's Desert Storm (Iraq), Provide Relief (Somalia, 1992–1993), Enduring Freedom (Afghanistan, 2001–), and Iraqi Freedom (Iraq, 2003–) have all been shouldered, planned, and executed by CENTCOM. This does not include responding to numerous regional terrorist threats, humanitarian relief efforts, and counterterrorism and counterinsurgency training missions with host nation security forces. Its early headquarters is pictured here in 1994. (Courtesy 6 AMW/HO.)

The idea for USSOCOM, which commands America's elite, multiservice units of irregular warfare specialists, began to permeate DoD and Congressional conversations following America's heroic yet tragic attempt to rescue the American hostages in Iran in 1980 (Operation Eagle Claw, or Desert One). SOCOM was subsequently activated on MacDill on April 16, 1987, in concert with REDCOM being disestablished, and SOCOM assumed REDCOM's facility, pictured here in 1987. (Courtesy 6 AMW/HO.)

Following the coup that overthrew Haiti's president Jean Bertrand Aristide, America intervened militarily under Operation Uphold Democracy. Pictured here in September 1994, MacDill AFB hosted over 70 C-130s from various bases to support operations in Haiti. Ideas to include the base in a round of closures had been overruled, partly because the operation again underscored MacDill's excellent strategic location. (Courtesy 6 AMW/HO.)

This Boeing KC-135R Stratotanker was visiting MacDill on April 12, 1996, as part of an air show display. Although still assigned to Malmstrom AFB's 43rd Air Refueling Group (ARG), a 1995 Defense Base Realignment and Closure Commission had ordered the 43rd to be deactivated and its 12 tankers, along with its subordinate unit, the 91st Aerial Refueling Squadron (ARS), to be transferred to MacDill. (Official USAF photograph; courtesy defenseimagery.mil.)

Following the 56th Tactical Fighter Wing's departure from MacDill, the base's host unit became the 6th Air Base Wing (ABW) on January 1, 1994, tasked with supporting MacDill's two combatant commands, USCENTCOM and USSOCOM, as well as NOAA aircraft and a multitude of tenant units. Boeing KC-135 Stratotankers, which would arrive later in 1996, can be seen along the flight line in the 1990s. (Courtesy 6 AMW/HO.)

With the arrival of the 91st ARS and its Stratotankers in 1996, the 6th ABW was redesignated the 6th Aerial Refueling Wing (ARW). This designation remained until January 1, 2001, when the 6th ARW was redesignated as the 6th Air Mobility Wing, an asset of the Air Force's Air Mobility Command (AMC). The 310th Airlift Squadron, with its Gulfstream V C-37As, was activated on the same date. (Courtesy 6 AMW/HO.)

Former US Special Operations Command (USSOCOM) commander Gen. Peter J. Schoomaker (US Army) is pictured giving a speech at the dedication ceremony of the Special Operations Memorial, located adjacent to SOCOM's main entrance on MacDill, on May 24, 1999. Schoomaker, a true warrior's warrior, served under Col. Charles A. Beckwith during the aforementioned Operation Eagle Claw. (Official USAF photograph; courtesy defenseimagery.mil.)

Guests admire the statue of the Special Operations Warrior unveiled on May 24, 1999. The memorial, sponsored by the Special Operations Memorial Foundation, was reconfigured in 2007 into the shape of SOCOM's spearhead. Standing tall and vigilant, the statue is surrounded by the names of those who have made the ultimate sacrifice, including Medal of Honor recipients. God bless them. (Official USAF photograph, courtesy defenseimagery.mil.)

www.arcadiapublishing.com

Discover books about the town where you grew up, the cities where your friends and families live, the town where your parents met, or even that retirement spot you've been dreaming about. Our Web site provides history lovers with exclusive deals, advanced notification about new titles, e-mail alerts of author events, and much more.

MADE IN THE USA

Arcadia Publishing, the leading local history publisher in the United States, is committed to making history accessible and meaningful through publishing books that celebrate and preserve the heritage of America's people and places. Consistent with our mission to preserve history on a local level, this book was printed in South Carolina on American-made paper and manufactured entirely in the United States.

This book carries the accredited Forest Stewardship Council (FSC) label and is printed on 100 percent FSC-certified paper. Products carrying the FSC label are independently certified to assure consumers that they come from forests that are managed to meet the social, economic, and ecological needs of present and future generations.

FSC

Mixed Sources
Product group from well-managed forests and other controlled sources

Cert no. SW-COC-001530
www.fsc.org
© 1996 Forest Stewardship Council

Find Your Place in History.